MW01194139

CONTENTS

BAHNSTORMER

The story of BMW motorcycles

L. J. K. Setright

TRANSPORT BOOKMAN PUBLICATIONS LTD

©1977   Transport Bookman Publications Ltd
Syon Park, Brentford
London, England TW8 8JF

ISBN 0 85184 021 3

Designed by
David Harris

Typeset by
Marian Pritchard & Associates

IBM Aldine Roman 12 on 13

Printed by
HGA Printing Company Ltd., Brentford, England

INTRODUCTION

If your familiarity with the Burtons of literature extends beyond the nineteenth-century Richard of *The Perfumed Garden* to the sixteenth-century Robert of *The Anatomy of Melancholy,* you may have encountered in the latter a reference to that thick, dark, Bavarian beer of which it was said

> *nil spissius illa dum bibitur*
> *nil clarius dum mingitur*
> *unde constat*
> *quod multas faeces in corpore linquat*

As might be expected of a Fellow of Brasenose College, Burton offered a translation that could hardly be bettered:

> Nothing goes in so thick;
> Nothing comes out as thin.
> It must needs follow, then,
> The dregs remain within.

What has thick dark Bavarian beer to do with BMW and motorcycles? The relationship is crucial: in the firm's car factories at Munich, the regular two-minute ring of the cash register is drowned by a great guzzling, sluicing, slurruping noise as the employees—most of them thick dark Bavarians—get on with their health-giving, morale-boosting task of downing a daily 1700 pints of Bavarian beer. So far as the true Bayerische Motoren Werke may be concerned, all is as it should be; but they make no motorcycles in Munich now. The two-wheeler factory is at Spandau, which is associated geographically with Berlin and historically with ordnance; and whatever the name-plate may say at the door, it is emphatically not a Bavarian motor works in style or substance.

Up here in the rigorous unromantic north, their critical faculties are not obscured by the flood of thick dark potables, nor their spirits weighed down by the dregs thereof. Munich may turn out hotted-up spivmobiles and tarted-up *Prunkwagen* but there has always been—and still is, if you are colourblind—an unmistakable sobriety about the motorcycles. In 1971 the Munich masters decreed that the motorcycles were to be dolled up in fancy chromium gewgaws to make them more attractive: but all that happened was a tide of blushing among the motorcycle sales staff, and a storm of protest from customers everywhere who wanted to know how much extra they should pay to have the previous year's model.

The people who buy BMW motorcycles are evidently tasteful and discriminating. And rich. They may no longer be inhibited by their former addiction to the sober city black-and-stripes that formerly distinguished the BMW from the harlequinade of common two-wheelers; but they accept now, as they have had to accept for the last twenty years, that there is nothing else besides the costly BMW to satisfy the Polonius/Brummel criteria for a gentleman's road-burner—rich but not gaudy, and as good as money can buy.

Other motorcycles are faster, flashier, noisier, thirstier and (with a couple of inconsiderable exceptions) cheaper. Some of them have better gearchanges. Nearly all of them are heavier and less comfortable for, as the age of the so-called superbikes has progressed, all the others have grown more implausibly massive while the BMW, twenty years ago one of the heaviest, has actually shed a few pounds and is now, throughout the range from 600 cc to the full-bloated litre, in almost every case the lightest of its capacity.

Better still, such weight as the BMW amounts to is hung low. That unique engine, with one big cylinder sticking out from each flank, inherits a tradition that goes back to 1923 if you look into Munich history, and further back still if you look outside; and it has not been proved wrong yet. It is not likely to be: there is no other way of making a two-cylinder four-stroke engine that is virtually perfectly balanced. When it is plonking along very slowly it can be felt pulsating, but the tingling vibration endemic among other big bangers is mercifully absent—and that is one of the reasons why the BMW can be ridden fast all day without fatigue of machine or rider.

Item by item, as we shall see in the unfolding of the story that follows, the true character of the BMW emerges: it is a sensible fast solo transport. It is something on which to cover long distances at high average speeds in unexpected comfort and with infallible reliability. It is something to buy and keep for years and years, not an evanescent plaything to be abandoned after a brief spell of trial and error. Other motorcycles may serve for a little recreation, a flurry of furious acceleration, flapping wheels, straining arms and overwhelmed ears, before they succumb to worn chains, burnt-out wiring or sudden severe shortage of roadholding. The BMW, because it too is fast and powerful, can also be ridden with the same sort of relish for the immediacies and intangibilities of motorcycling: when the tyres and brakes and handlebars are right, it can be ridden very hard indeed.

Even then it will last for a long time, will go on and on giving of its best when others might inspire their riders to fear the worst. It is in every sense the heir to a long-lasting tradition. An important part of that tradition is that the sustained ability to go and steer and stop should be complemented by all the other facilities a gentleman rider needs, including the ability to sail into the forecourt of the most discriminating hotel or restaurant without causing eyebrow or nose to be raised. It does not merely look quiet, it is quiet. Above all it is an exceptionally well-bred motorcycle: it is not for nothing that BMWs and their riders have been called the silent minority. To appear civilised is difficult for a motorcycle; but the BMW does it, and is unique in having done it for a very long time.

We shall have to consider what made it so—whether it was the genius of engineers or the cunning of salesmen, whether it came about by sociological deliberation or historical accident, whether it was demanded by the customers or imposed by the limitations of the basic design. This quality of civilisation is one that is difficult to define; but the art historian, Sir Kenneth Clark, has made an interesting attempt. Here is not the place in this book to examine his conclusions, but it is an appropriate one at which to recall some of his premises: *Civilisation means something more than energy and will and creative power . . .*

CHAPTER 1

THE DIE IS CAST

The man who designed the first BMW motorcycle, Max Friz, was unquestionably blessed with creative power; but the energy and will were lacking. He did not want to design motorcycles. He did not like motorcycles. It was not to get involved with these messy rut-bound stinkwheels that he had set himself up as an engineer: he was a committed aviation enthusiast, and an aero-engine designer of proven talent. The management could urge him to design a motorcycle until they went blue in the face: in his unheated office in the keen Bavarian winter, he was blue in the fingers.

The first aircraft to be built in Germany flew only in 1909; but there was a Circuit of Germany race the next year for a prize fund of 50,000 Marks, and in 1911 a Mercédès aero-engine was awarded the first prize of the Society of Automobile and Aeronautical Engineers. The Mercédès engines were built by Daimler, who had been at it tentatively for at least a couple of years; but their 1911 engine was definitive, embodying a form of construction that was to set the pattern for many manufacturers to follow for decades to come. The technique was one that Daimler had used as early as 1906, in a car engine that in turn owed its inspiration to a Panhard of 1903, and involved building separate steel cylinders with welded-on sheet metal water jackets, all mounted in line on a common crankcase. The firm was, of course, founded by Gottlieb Daimler, who shared with Karl Benz the distinction of being one of the founders of the automobile industry. The man who paved the way for them by creating the four-stroke engine, Nikolaus August Otto, had a son who came into the German aviation picture in that same year of 1911, when he set up a firm called the Gustav Otto Flugmaschinenfabrik Munchen; its premises were at the eastern end of the Oberweisenfeld

Airport at Munich; and the site is occupied by the BMW head-quarters today.

In 1911 BMW did not exist, but the circumstances that gave it birth were evolving, and around Munich the constituents that made it were gradually assembling. The development of aero-engines in Germany was at this time more or less in the hands of private enterprise, the government taking a somewhat reactionary view of the whole affair. Nevertheless there were ways of encouraging them, and on the birthday of the Kaiser, in January 1912, it was announced that he had offered a prize for the best German aero-engine to be presented a year later.

We can ignore the terms of the competition, interesting though they were. We can ignore the fact that Daimler won second prize with their six-cylinder engine; and we can certainly ignore the fact that Benz won first prize with a four-cylinder affair, since nobody ordered it, the machine having proved to be distressingly vibratory. The thing we should note is that the German motor industry flung itself so enthusiastically into this competition for the *Kaiserpreis* that a total of twenty-six firms entered no less than forty-four different engines. We might also note that this was the time when young Max Friz built his first effective aero-engine, even if he did not figure among the prizewinners.

Seeing what a dreadful flop the winning Benz engine was, to have lost the competition was not necessarily a disgrace; but because the Benz flopped, to come second was effectively to win, and the six-cylinder Daimler founded a German school of aero-engine design that was to be crushingly successful in the years soon to come. Most manufacturers were aware of the impossibility of achieving perfect balance with an in-line four-cylinder engine, and a large number of European manufacturers avoided the issue by cultivating the elegant and smooth-running rotary—which was fine until they wanted more power, when the shortcomings of the rotary began to appear both transitively and intransitively fatal. The Germans, unwittingly trading problems of balance for problems of torsional vibration in the crank-shaft, were more inclined to pursue smooth running by adopting the six-cylinders-in-line configuration, and most of their examples worked very well—not only those of Daimler and Benz and Austro-Daimler, but also particularly those of Rapp who set up the Rapp Motoren Werke in 1913. Three years later, Karl Rapp and Max Friz combined as founders of the Bayerische Flugzeugwerke AG, with a capital of 200,000 Reichsmarks, and with premises on the north side of Munich.

Their exclusive stock-in-trade was aero-engines which, amongst other distinctions, earned praise from Baron Manfred von Richthofen whose fighter squadron was equipped with them. In fact the first victim of this particularly chivalrous officer only fell in September of that same year; within twelve months, by which time the Baron had sent down perhaps thirty or forty foes, Rapp and Friz had put up five hundred BFW engines. A coalition of the interests of Bayerische Flugzeugwerke and Gustav Otto Flugmaschinenfabrik led to the foundation of a new company, the Bayerische Motoren Werke GmbH, to be reconstituted on 13 August 1918 with the name and *Aktiengesellschaft* status that it has enjoyed to this day: Bayerische Motoren Werke AG. Its capital was 12,000,000 Marks, it employed 3,500 people, and the shareholders asked a Viennese, Franz Joseph Popp, to be sole director.

Popp was then 32 years old, a reserve officer in the old Austro-Hungarian Marines who had wanted to be a journalist. He was keen on motoring and aviation, had graduated from Brunn as an electrical and civil engineer, and until joining BMW was head of the department of electrical railways and locomotives. The Popp period at BMW lasted longer than any other rule, until 1940; but one of his first moves was one of his most decisive. Friz had been refused a 450 DM salary at Daimler; Popp saw that he got it at BMW as engine designer.

In the newly constituted BMW factory, work was well under way with its first high-altitude engine, a water-cooled in-line six developing 185 horsepower. This was soon succeeded by the mark 4 of 250 horsepower, an engine that was interesting because although it was German and designed for flying high, it was unsupercharged. The Germans were undoubtedly the first successful exponents of super-charging, being the first to appreciate the practical advantages of the superior height that forced induction allowed; but this was not their only method of achieving power at height. They were also in advance of the rest of the world in building quite light engines with unusually high compression ratios, accepting that the engines had to be partially throttled at low altitudes; and this was the particular *forte* of BMW.

They might have achieved even more than they did, but in 1919 aero-engine production was forced to a halt by the terms of the Treaty of Versailles. Rapp and Friz, with their passionate devotion to aviation, could not bear to abandon their project just when it was ready to be put to the proof, so they carried on their tests in secret. They were eminently successful: in two flights in May and June, 1919, Franz Diemer piloted a BMW-engined DFW biplane to new world record altitudes culminating in a climb of 9760 metres (32,030 ft) – and the Allied Commission of Control promptly confiscated all the documents pertaining to the record. What they could not take away from the man most intimately concerned, Friz, was the sense of achievement and of vocation that the success had given him, and the confidence that naturally followed.

It is no good being good at your job, and knowing that you are good at it, if you are not allowed to do it. With so many workers and stockholders to support, BMW had to find something else to do, and demeaned themselves with the production of air brakes and agricultural machinery. They did the industrial equivalent of taking in other people's washing, their foundry producing castings for other companies. They used the sheet metal and plywood stocks left over from aircraft production to make tool boxes and office furniture, and so they struggled on; but by 1920 they had to enlarge their share capital to 24,000,000 Marks.

How does that pilot's poem go? *Shed no tears for Johnny head-in-air . . .* Friz still had his heart up there, but times were hard and he had to get his feet on the ground, however dull the work. He designed a 45/60 horsepower marine engine, a water-cooled four-cylinder affair that could also be used for lorries or as a stationary engine. The company's salvation clearly lay in diversification; so, however reluctantly, they involved themselves in the motorcycle business too. Their first effort was a lightweight one with a single-cylinder two-stroke engine of 146 cc displacement. They called it the Flink.

It was of no consequence except as a means of entry into the motorcycle market. Their next two-wheeler was to be the Helios, fashioned on the pattern of an early Douglas with a horizontally-opposed two-cylinder air-cooled side-valve engine mounted length-wise (that is, with its crankshaft athwart the frame) and rather high with a belt drive to the rear wheel. Friz despised it.

The management urged him to do better. As another year went by, the company's activities had become dominated by air brake production, and their principal contractor Knorr-Bremse AG acquired ninety per cent of the share capital. Engine production stagnated, but in a bid for revival BMW paid 75,000,000 Marks for the property of BFW and decided to increase their capital to 120,000,000 Marks. Meanwhile Friz had been doing some thinking.

He had been thinking about that flat twin. Maybe he was schooled in the water-cooled-six tradition, but an air-cooled horizontally-opposed engine made much better sense in this weird new motor-cycling context with which he was becoming familiar. This layout ensured smooth torque, perfect primary balance and (provided that the two cylinders were not unduly offset relative to each other to accommodate overlap of the connecting rods) almost perfect secondary balance with only a slight rocking couple.

Such an engine is particularly attractive for installation in a motor-cycle: if arranged so that the cylinders are in the transverse plane they project into the air stream and are guaranteed a sufficiency of cooling air, while if they are disposed fore and aft to simplify the transmission they can still be arranged low down so as to give the bicycle a low centre of gravity and so endow it with basically good handling potential. Douglas had been doing this in Bristol since 1906, basing their designs on the work of Barter whose similar engine had originally gone into a machine called the Fairy or Fée. Even that had not been the first, for there was the Barry in 1904; but it was the Douglas that had really established the idea, which had grown immeasurably more popular during the Great War thanks to its exploits between the knees of many a British army despatch rider.

All this history—and more—is worth recalling, if only to discredit those German journalists who have pronounced that the M2B15 engine that Friz produced in 1922 was the first air-cooled horizontally-opposed engine. It was nothing of the sort; but it was the first significant BMW motorcycle engine. It had a displacement of 500 cc and an output of 6.5 horsepower, and when BMW sold it in quantities to Victoria (the Nürnberg motorcycle manufacturers, no relations to the even older firm of the same name in Glasgow) it proudly bore the BMW badge.

It is one of the cleverest and best-known badges in the business. It is basically a circle quartered into alternating blue and white segments. When the sky is clear and the light is right and the two-bladed airscrew is spinning well, it is the picture an airman sees when he looks through the airscrew's arc. *Shed no tears for Johnny head-in-air* . . . the company's tide was just about to turn.

They installed a stove in the office of Friz. Legend has it that it made all the difference: maybe it did, or maybe it was just coincidence, but shortly afterwards this man who professed disdain for motor-cycles produced a design which in one magnificent and beautifully co-ordinated gesture ushered the motorcycle into a new era. It was not the world's first tolerably modern motorcycle: England had already given us the Scott, which for decades proved itself inimitable, and the ABC which the unimaginative English public found implaus-ible. The new BMW, to be known as the R32, was nevertheless at least as outstanding in concept as either of them: it founded a new German school of design, it established a BMW tradition destined to survive unbroken from 1923 until today, it injected a measure of civilisation into an activity that had always shown a tinge of barbarity, and it put BMW back on their feet.

Perhaps it did have rather a lot in common with Granville Bradshaw's ABC. It is said that some visitors from BMW were seen on the ABC stand at the 1919 Olympia Motor Cycle Show in London, intently studying and carefully sketching the features that made it so outstanding. The engine was a flat twin set with its overhead-valved cylinders across a remarkably modern-looking cradle frame. Built along car lines, the transmission comprised a plate clutch fitting on to the back of the engine's enclosed flywheel and linking it to a four-speed gearbox that had a car-type gate-change gearlever.

Indeed, the only concessions to contemporary motorcycle practice seemed to be the presence of a wheel at each end of the bicycle and chain drive from the gearbox to the rear hub. The frame was sprung front and rear, there were internal expanding drum brakes on both wheels, and there was even a measure of protection against the weather. The machine had proved itself fast, light and stable; but it never proved itself commercially.

What was the trouble? James Sheldon said of the ABC that *Only Bradshaw could have designed it, only Ford could have organised its production, and only Morris could have sold it on the scale necessary for financial success.* The BMW R32 was at least as heterodox, but Friz and Popp between them did all that was necessary. The machine was the rage of the 1923 Paris Show, and not only because the transverse-twin engine was coupled to a car-type clutch and gearbox. What came next was scarcely less significant, for the connexion between gearbox and rear hub was made by shaft drive and final bevel gears. This was sophistication indeed: apart from the abominably crude shaft with exposed bevels of the early FN, practically every motorcycle then used chains—undoubtedly remarkably efficient when clean, new, and nicely lubricated, but in their exposed condition hardly likely to enjoy these circumstances for more than a few miles. To be sure, a few motorcycles such as the Sunbeam had extensive enclosure of the transmission chains, sometimes merely as protection against the dust and rain, sometimes serving as oil baths to maintain copious lubrication of the many overworked plain bearings of which a roller chain is comprised. These enclosures, however, had proved unpopular: they rattled, they got in the way when a wheel change was necessary (as it often was, tyres being as treacherous as they then were), they did not look sporty enough. Whatever the objection to them, they went; but with the BMW shaft drive there were no such problems. The gears built into the rear hub might not display the same high mechanical efficiency as could a chain, but such efficiency as they had they kept. Better still, by incorporating a readily removable wheel spindle, Friz made the job of detaching the rear wheel quicker and easier and cleaner than it had ever been.

Nor was this the limit of his genius. A duplex tubular frame gave the R32 uncommon lateral and torsional stiffness. Short trailing links at the bottom of the front forks reduced the front unsprung mass to the barest minimum. If the ABC and one or two other 'bikes had four-speed transmission, whereas the R32 like the majority of others had only a three-speed gearbox, it made up the deficiency by being above average in power: Friz had redesigned his original flat twin quite extensively, and in the process of turning it through ninety degrees to expose its cylinders to more effective draughts of cooling air he had been able to increase its output to 8.5 horsepower. By the standards of the time this gave quite a decent performance, even if by those same standards the stovepipe-framed R32 was not considered light at 270 lb. The brakes to stop it were not exactly exciting either: at the front was an internal expanding drum brake, but Friz had not yet worked out how to incorporate one of these in his bevel-drive rear hub, contenting himself with an old-fashioned vee-block pressed into a dummy pulley.

The average customer's eyes never strayed as far as these extremities, being riveted by the attractions of what lay between them. For 1923 it was a remarkably clean and well integrated design. The crankcase, the timing cover, the gearbox, the sump and the ski-shaped foot-boards all seemed to be parts of the same almost monolithic piece of aluminium foundrywork. The two forward-facing exhausts disappeared underneath into a very compact silencer, while from the rear of each side-valved cylinder an inlet pipe curved up and inwards to the neat central twin-barrel carburettor, nicely accessible but out of harm's way on top of the gearbox.

However mellifluous its inlet manifolding, a 500 cc side-valve engine with a compression ratio of only 5 to 1 and a maximum output of 8.5 horsepower at a mere 3300 rpm could not, when driving through a wide-ratio three-speed gearbox, hope to make this robust 270-pounder a ball of fire. In fact its maximum speed was only 90 km/h (56 mph), and in international competition it would have been murdered by much less substantial, less pretentious (and in the long run less significant) but more efficient sporting devices such as the six-speed 350 cc AJS. For the Germans, however, grunting under the fardels of the vengeful Versailles Treaty, there was precious little international competition; and at home the R32 was good enough to carry Franz Bieber to victory in the 1924 German road-racing championship. Competition successes such as this were nevertheless the effect rather than the cause of the machine's popularity; such a beautiful design could not fail to be successful when its appearance was so timely.

Germany was not the only country then suffering depression. Their conquerors, having retired to both sides of the Atlantic to dress their wounds and relieve their frustrations, had enjoyed an immediate industrial boom that had done wonders for such markets as the one for luxury cars, whereas the aviation industry was left to rot until such time as the vast post-war surplus stocks of engines and airframes had been consumed. By 1921 that first wave of careless optimism had subsided, and what had been a boom was now little more than an emptily muttering echo. Even Rolls-Royce, growing fast in size and reputation, were tempted to think that the odd twenty or thirty thousand pounds they might get from the British government on an aero-engine contract might be well worth having. Even France, above other nations insistent on retribution, was forced to realise that only harm could come from grinding Germany's economy finally into the dust: and by 1924 restrictions on aircraft engine production were lifted to allow BMW to get back into the business. Suddenly the prospects for BMW were rosy: depression in the car market would keep the motorcycle market busy (3100 examples of the R32 were built in its three-year production span) and Max Friz could get back to his precious aero-engines.

He did this by continuing work on his 33-litre water-cooled in-line six. The restrictions had not been lifted in their entirety, continuing to forbid the Germans to build really powerful aero-engines, but this BMW with 250 to 310 horsepower at its disposal was enough to gather a dazzling succession of world records, culminating in no fewer than twenty-two established in 1927. The lessons learnt with this were not wasted, and a new breed of liquid-cooled V12s of roughly double the size and power were to make their appearance in the 1930s, powering aircraft such as those with which Lufthansa set up their remarkable express postal service between Berlin and South America.

Were the motorcycles therefore to be demoted to the status of a second-class interest in the factory? Friz might be in no doubt about his order of priorities, but he had called the tune and there was no shortage of earnest and devoted young engineers ready to play it. In particular he had a protégé by the name of Rudolph Schleicher who was to take over the day-to-day engineering and the design and development division, a man whose abilities as a rider usefully supplemented his gifts as an engineer.

Things were looking up. At the company's General Meeting, shareholders were told that the number of employees was now 1200 and that it would be opportune to convert the inflationary paper market capital of 160,000,000 Marks to 3,000,000 Marks. With reserves of nearly 400,000 Marks and a turnover of 8,300,000, it looked healthy enough for the shareholders to receive a ten per cent dividend.

This optimism was confirmed in 1925 when the stock capital was raised again to 5,000,000 Marks, when the turnover increased to 15,000,000 in notably higher proportion than the increase in the number of employees. The number of models of motorcycle offered to the public was also increased: the same year saw the first overhead-valve sports model, the R37, leave the works. Essentially similar to the R32, it was distinguished by big elliptical rocker boxes shrouding pushrod-operated overhead valves, sufficient (with an increase in compression ratio) almost to double the output of the engine. The maximum speed in standard trim was raised to 115 km/h (71 mph) and with a little suitable attention the machine could be ridden to good purpose in competition events. In 1925 BMW riders won ninety-one races in European competition, including the German Grand Prix.

The factory was not catering only for hard men and tearaways. 1925 also saw the introduction of the R39, first in a long line of single-cylinder motorcycles best considered separately; and by thus catering for the utility, touring and sporting sectors of the market, having firmly and amazingly quickly established themselves as manufacturers of high repute—thanks to the goaded imagination and ability of Max Friz (or was it the stove?) everything was set fair for their future profitability. In 1926 their turnover was 9,000,000

Marks, the shareholders enjoyed a 12 per cent dividend, while the factory began to look abroad for more opportunities to preach its very particular motorcycling gospel.

They had realised that there was a lot to be learned from competition, just as in terms of publicity and sales there was a lot to be earned by it. It produced results more quickly, with its hot-house influence on development—especially when a company had men who could garner experience at first hand by riding the machine themselves and then apply the lessons learned directly to the drawing board or production line. Such were the ambitions that impelled Schleicher to enter an R37 in the 1926 International Six Days Trial— the most gruelling in motorcycle sport. It was to take place in England, where the industry and the sport flourished alike with an intensity unrivalled anywhere else in the world, and in an atmosphere of flagrant nationalism supported by a generally indisputable superiority. Despite all this, and despite tyres that were hardly suitable for the unfamiliar terrain of the event, Schleicher won the first gold medal ever to be awarded to a German on British soil.

This outstanding victory prompted generous praise from the pen of Professor A.M. Low, then technical director of the Auto-cycle Union which was the governing body of the sport in Britain: *The most interesting machine of the whole meeting was undoubtedly the German BMW. A horizontally opposed two-cylinder engine which is mounted transversely in the frame—with completely enclosed valve gear, block construction and shaft drive. Even after the hardest days there wasn't a bit of oil to be seen anywhere, the machine was beautifully quiet and seemed to have an enormous power reserve. It is miles ahead of any British machine as far as design is concerned.*

The R37 had a short life, with the smallest production run (175) of all commercially produced models in the company's motorcycling history. In 1926 the two twins were replaced by the side-valve R42 and the sporting overhead-valve R47. Both enjoyed a boost in power, notably the side-valver which had a removable light-alloy cylinder head and forward-facing cooling fins. Both machines lost the primitive block-and-pulley brake on the rear wheel, which was replaced by a transmission brake supposed to have its effect multiplied by the mechanical advantage of the final drive bevel gears, for it was a band brake on the drive shaft at the output from the gearbox. Another refinement was a relocation of the speedometer: it was now set in the top of the fuel tank, and the bare drive cable was led from it to the gearbox.

More development was evident in the R52 and R57 which came along in 1928. The brakes were larger, notably at the front, the exhaust systems included full-length tail pipes with small fishtails at the ends, and there was a new three-speed gearbox with oil lubrication in place of the old grease-filled one. By this time BMW had 1500 employees and were running very profitably; and as if to prove the expansiveness of their mood they introduced the first 750 cc twins, the R62 and R63, the latter with a resounding 24 horsepower and 75 mph performance.

It was interesting that the ohv versions were no longer merely modifications of the side-valvers. Prior to the R52 all BMW motor-cycles had a piston stroke of 68 mm, identical to the cylinder bore; but now it was recognized by their engineers that where power was sought (as in the ohv engines) a large piston area was desirable, and that where low-speed flexibility was sought (as in the side-valve engines) a low ratio of bore to stroke would be desirable. Thus the R52 and R62 both had crankshafts giving a stroke of 78 mm, the bores being 63 and 78 mm respectively; the sporting versions, the R57 and R63, maintained the old 68 mm stroke with bores of 68 and 83 mm.

How well the 1.22:1 bore:stroke ratio fitted the R63 engine for further development became apparent when the machine was made the basis for a record-breaker with which Ernst Henne was to become a setter of astonishingly prolific new standards. He began in 1929 by setting the world motorcycle speed record at 216.8 km/h (134.6 mph). He was still riding the blown 750 cc record-breaker, in its final highly tuned and elegantly streamlined form, in 1935 when he raised the record (for the sixth time) to 256.1 km/h (159.2 mph), having in the interval also set two world speed records for three-wheelers by the simple expedient of tacking a vestigial pseudo-sidecar on to one flank of the big BMW.

Something far more important than a fifty per cent increase in engine size happened in 1928. The company decided to go into car manufacture, and for this purpose acquired the production facilities of Dixi in Eisenach. They also bought (presumably for rather less, since the Eisenach deal cost them 2.2 million Marks) a licence to manufacture a left-hand-drive version of the Austin 7 car, and generally took on obligations amounting to 7.8 million Marks. Their obligations to the bank soared as cars went into production in 1929, though they still paid a seven per cent dividend; and it was only to be expected that this expansion of the company's interests and burdens would be reflected in motorcycle design or production. So it proved: while Ernst Henne was running up one record after another on private tracks and on public roads, engineers were applying constructional techniques already familiar in the car industry to the motorcycle. The age of pressed steel had arrived.

Obviously, BMW had manufacturing facilities at Eisenach that it needed to employ profitably rather than let lie idle while the production of cars was organised. Equally obviously, they were anxious to rationalise the engineering work carried out at Eisenach and Munich. Less obviously, they were genuinly interested in the possibilities of pressed steel, which when used intelligently can be built up into structures of much greater stiffness than could be achieved by the methods then considered orthodox. The pioneer of this work was an American, Edward Gowan Budd, born in 1870, who had begun to study pressed steel and its uses in 1899 after reading mechanical engineering at the Franklyn Institute in Philadelphia. For a while he worked on railway rolling stock, at the same time making a study of current and potential welding techniques on which the fruition of his ideas would depend. Finally, in 1912 he set up his own company and embarked on a crusade to popularise the all-steel body for the motor car. He succeeded—most notably with the famous Budd-bodied Dodge of 1916—and by 1924 his work had extended overseas to include a collaboration with André Citroën, who had earlier been fired by the mass production techniques of Henry Ford and had set up the first similar factory in Europe. Budd's expertise was widely recognized, and the companies who employed him as a consultant included BMW.

Such was the background to the introduction in 1929 of the pressed steel frame in the new R11 and R16 motorcycles from Munich. It was known colloquially as the Star frame, and its most notable feature was the broad and generous gussetting that supported the steering head and embraced the newly curvaceous petrol tank. Equally neat and similarly superior frame engineering could be seen where the final drive bevel box and hub were fitted into the pressed steel loops at the rear of the chassis, and in the elegant beams that constituted the front forks, still bearing trailing bottom-link and leaf-spring suspension. It was altogether a great advance, notably stiffer in torsion than the earlier tubular frames and destined to remain in production till the end of 1934.

There were other refinements too. For the first time, a motor-cycle had floating wheel spindles at the front and rear, improving the location and easing the removal of either wheel. Also for the first time, the motorcycle was delivered ready for the road with complete lighting equipment, horn, and speedometer, which hitherto had conventionally been treated as extras by the trade. Continued development led to the BMW carburettor being replaced, first by a Sum multiple-jet device, later by a pair of Amal instruments. The gears providing drive and timing for the camshaft and ignition were replaced by sprockets and a chain. The gearchange (alas, it was still a three-speeder) was made easier to operate through a neat gate-type shift which nestled behind the right knee pad, and the transmission was further refined by a split drive shaft, flexible couplings taking the place of the original one-piece drive shaft. There were even air filters for the carburettors, and in every respect the latest BMW motor-cycles displayed the refinement, luxury, advanced technology and ample performance that should have earned the company sales as formidable as its reputation. Alas, it was all rather untimely: the new Star-framed BMWs were born into a period of economic crisis.

The same had been true of the R32, which had been presented to the world when the financial measures of the Weimar Republic (founded in 1919) had ended in tragic failure. When the old German Empire, the Second Reich, had fallen in 1918, the currency had already been inflated; but under the terms of the peace treaty of 1919 Germany lost an eighth of its European land area, with 6½ million people, all of its colonies and foreign investments, its merchant marine, and much of its material resources, after which it had to sign a blank reparations cheque. In this situation the republic had to export its gold reserves to pay for food, since it could not export manufactured products or borrow money. The inevitable result was a precipitous fall in the value of the Mark: in the autumn of 1923, the Mark was quoted in Cologne at 12,000 million to the dollar. The economic foundation of the powerful German middle class had been destroyed, and panic fiscal measures had to be taken to check complete dissolution. No wonder the BMW management, presumably foreseeing this with as much foreboding as others in the thick of it, had been urging Friz to think of something good.

Whether the R32 would have been good enough to save the company, without the economic changes made at international level the following year, is very doubtful. The resurgence of BMW undoubtedly dated from the time of the R32, but even such a brilliant design as this would not alone have checked the company's fall. In fact it was economic adjustment associated with American loans that brought on an artificial era of prosperity between 1924 and 1929, an era in which any potentially expansive industry had a good chance of flourishing, as BMW did.

1929 was when the pendulum swung, although a company might not feel the full reversal of it until the following year. With effect from the autumn of '29, the terms of the Young Plan required Germany to begin annual reparation payments of more than 2,000 million Marks a year, to be kept up until 1967: the political turmoil inspired by this marked the beginning of the decline of the Weimar Republic. Was this the time to bring out brave new motorcycle designs, let alone to venture into car production? Was it the time for BMW to increase their bank obligations to 15 million Marks, and to take on more employees to expand the payroll to 3860?

It was the time, as they realised in the following year, to produce something really cheap to take advantage of the tax concessions for motorcycles under 200 cc capacity. So, whilst the mighty 750 on which Ernst Henne had raised the speed record to 221.5 km/h (137.7 mph) earlier in the year was displayed proudly on the BMW stand at the 1930 Paris Salon, the engineers back at the factory were working on their *Volksmotorrad,* a 200 cc single, the smallest and most utilitarian since the Flink. While they were planning it, the economic crisis was reducing the company's turnover by about ten per cent, which enforced the dismissal of about seven hundred employees.

By 1932 the turnover had dropped to the lowest since 1928, despite the fact that new cars were going into series production. The crisis was not restricted to the company nor even to the nation: it was by now world wide, as the slump wave spread out from its Wall Street epicentre. Amongst other desperate measures, the German government suspended vehicle taxation, with the predictable result that there was a run on the purchase of motorcycles—and if the people were going to buy motorcycles, there was plenty of encouragement for them to buy from BMW. The firm's prowess had been continually demonstrated in assorted sporting and other ventures, including trans-atlantic flights, world speed records, and successes in the Monte Carlo Rally, while the motorcycles collected twenty-two gold medals in the 1931 Harz 3 Days event, the most demanding endurance trial in the national calendar. As for Ernst Henne, he was still at it with the 750, its flanks smoothed by sheet metal enclosures, its engine tuned to ever higher degrees, and its rider progressively streamlined with comical aluminium fairings attached to his helmet and posterior to bring the drag down and help the speed up. By 1932 the absolute world record for two-wheelers had been lifted to 244.4 km/h (151.9 mph), and for three-wheelers to 207.7 (129.1)—and to silence objections that there was more to motorcycling than high straight-line speed and mountain climbing, there were triumphs in such events as the Targa Florio, the German and Hungarian Grands Prix, and domestic races and sprints in profusion. Already there were some well established riders associated with BMW, not only Henne but also Hans Soenius and Karl Gall.

If the effort put into this sort of publicity bore any true relationship to the increase in sales that followed, it was effort well expended. The boom that motorcycling had enjoyed in the mid-1920s might have been artificial, a reflection of the depression that inhibited the customers from buying cars instead; but now BMW were flourishing again. Especially in aviation their interests were quickening, and to back up their experience with water-cooled aero-engines they took out a licence to manufacture some air-cooled radials. The chosen models were of American origin, interestingly reflecting the degree to which German recovery had been funded by American capital, for at this time the most popular air-cooled radial by far, an aero-engine so highly esteemed that it was licensed for manufacture in fourteen countries, was England's Bristol Jupiter. Be that as it may, BMW chose the Pratt & Whitney Hornet and Wasp engines, the former going into the new and in every way remarkable trimotor transport, the Junkers JU52.

Things were looking up: despite the surrounding gloom, a new wave of optimism appeared in Germany following the elections of July 1932, and at the end of January the following year the old Weimar Republic was finished. In its place was born the Third Reich, the empire that was to last for a thousand years but instead consumed millions of people.

The millions that mattered to BMW at this critical point in their evolution were written in Marks on the paper of the newly stabilised currency. Turnover in 1933 shot up to 33 million Marks, the payroll to 4720, and the company even paid a six per cent dividend. At the end of 1934 BMW employed 12576 people turning out engines and road vehicles worth 82 million Marks. In a year their motorcycles had earned more than a hundred first and second places in competition, and Henne had gone faster still. The workers were riding the R2, the soldiers the R4, traditionalists the R11 and the sportsmen the R16, and a cursory look at any of these machines would immediately inspire recollection of the seminal design of 1923. It was time for something new.

	R32	R37	R42
ENGINE Type Number	M2B33	M2B36	M43
Cylinders, bore, stroke mm	2x68x68	2x68x68	2x68x68
Displacement cm^3	494	494	494
Compression ratio :1	5	6.2	4.9
Valve location	S	oh	S
Camshaft	1	1	1
Carburettor	1 BMW	1 BMW	1 BMW
Power PS max	8.5	16	12
at rev/min	3300	4000	3400
Corresponding bmep kg/cm^2	4.76	7.39	6.52
Oil capacity, litres	2	2	2
TRANSMISSION Type Number	G34	G34	G44
Gear ratios :1 i	2.11	2.11	2.34
top gear ii	1.40	1.40	1.40
iii	1	1	1
Final drive ratio :1	4.4 or 5.36	4.4 or 5.36	4.5 or 6.3*
CHASSIS Type Number	R32	R37	R42
Frame	tubular	tubular	tubular
Front forks	trailing link	trailing link	trailing link
springing	leaf	leaf	leaf
damping	friction	friction	friction
Rear forks	unsprung	unsprung	unsprung
Front brake type	drum 1LS	drum 1LS	drum 1LS
diameter mm	150	150	150
Rear brake type	V-block	V-block	band on transmission drum
Tyres	26x3	26x3	27x2.75 or 26x3.5
Fuel tank, litres	14	14	14
Weight, kg	120	134	126
Maximum speed km/h	95-100	115	95
Frame Numbers	1001-4100	100-275	10001-16999
Engine Numbers	31000-34100	35001-35175	40001-46999
Quantity built	3100	175	6900
Years of Production	1923—6	1925—6	1926—8

*3.8 or 5.7 from frame 11401

	R62	R63	R11
ENGINE Type Number	M56 SI	M60 SI	M56
Cylinders, bore, stroke mm	2x78x78	2x83x68	2x78x78
Displacement cm^3	745	734	745
Compression ratio :1	5.5	6.2	5.5
Valve location	S	oh	S
Carburettor	1 BMW	1 BMW	1
Power PS max	18	24	18
at rev/min	3400	4000	3400
Corresponding bmep kg/cm^2	5.51	7.46	5.51
Oil capacity, litres	2	2	2.5
TRANSMISSION Type Number	G56 S1	G56 S1	G56
Gear ratios :1 i	2.58	2.58	2.61
top gear ii	1.42	1.42	1.43
iii	1	1	1
Final drive ratio :1	4.05 or 4.75		4.45 or 5.18
CHASSIS Type Number	F56	F56	'Star'
Frame	tubular	tubular	pressed steel
Tyres	26x3.5 or 3.25	26x3.5 or 3.25	26x3.5 or 3.25
Fuel tank, litres	12.5	12.5	14
Weight, kg	155	155	162
Maximum speed km/h	115	115-120	100
Engine Numbers	60001-73984	75001-76156	
Quantity built	4000	1000	8300
Years of Production	1928—9	1928—9	1929—34

	R47	R52	R57
ENGINE Type Number	M51	M57	M59
Cylinders, bore, stroke mm	2x68x68	2x78x63	2x68x68
Displacement cm^3	494	487	494
Compression ratio :1	5.8	5	5.8
Valve location	oh	S	oh
Camshaft	1	1	1
Carburettor	1 BMW	1 BMW	1 BMW
Power PS max	18	12	18
at rev/min	4000	3400	4000
Corresponding bmep kg/cm^2	8.31	6.62	8.31
Oil capacity, litres	2	2	2.5
TRANSMISSION Type Number	G44	G56 S1	G56 S1
Gear Ratios :1　　　　i	2.34	2.58	2.58
top gear　　　　　　　ii	1.40	1.42	1.42
iii	1	1	1
Final drive ratio :1	4.4 or 5.7	4.75 or 5.7	4.75 or 5.7
CHASSIS Type Number	R47	F56	F56
Frame	tubular	tubular	tubular
Front forks	trailing link	trailing link	trailing link
springing	leaf	leaf	leaf
damping	friction	friction	friction
Rear Forks	unsprung	unsprung	unsprung
Front brake type	drum 1LS	drum 1LS	drum 1LS
diameter mm	150	200	200
Rear Brake type		band on transmission drum	
Tyres	27x3.5 or 26x3	26x3.5	26x3.5
Fuel tank, litres	14	12.5	12.5
Weight, kg	130	152	150
Maximum speed km/h	110	100	115
Frame numbers	4201-5999	20000-30600	20000-30600
Engine numbers	34201-35999	47001-51383	70001-71012
Quantity built	1700	9000	10000
Years of production	1927–8	1928–9	1928–30

R16

ENGINE Type Number		M60
Cylinders, bore, stroke mm		2x83x68
Displacement cm^3		734
Compression ratio :1		6.5
Valve location		oh
Camshaft		1
Carburettor		1 BMW
Power PS max		25
at rev/min		4000
Corresponding bmep kg/cm^2		7.77
Oil capacity, litres		2.5
TRANSMISSION Type Number		G56
Gear Ratios :1	i	2.61
	ii	1.43
	iii	1
Final drive ratio :1		4.45 or 5.18
CHASSIS Type Number		F66
Frame		pressed steel
Front forks		trailing link
springing		leaf
damping		friction
Rear forks		unsprung
Front brake type		drum 1LS
diameter mm		200
Rear brake type		band on transmission drum
Tyres		26x3.5 or 3.25
Fuel tank, litres		14
Weight, kg		165
Maximum speed km/h		120
Frame Numbers		20000-30600
Engine Numbers		75001-76156
Quantity built		1900
Years of production		1929-34

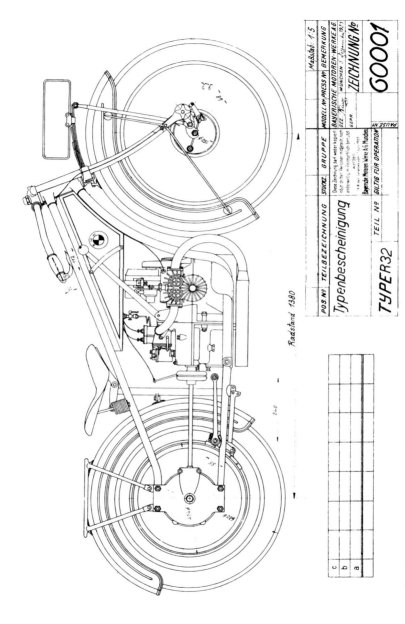

Not the first BMW motorcycle, but the first to matter: the R32 in a general arrangement drawing, dated somewhat later than the machine appeared.

The addition of lights and speedometer quite altered the racy looks of the basic R32.

R37

Young Rudolf Schleicher with his competition R37.

The original trailing-link forks
offered little lateral stiffness. How
sensible, on the other hand, appear
those ski-shaped footboards.

R42

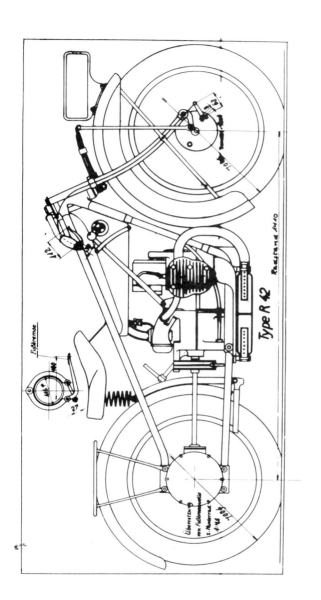

The detail above the saddle on this R42 drawing shows the footbrake, mounted on the drive shaft and operated by the rider's heel.

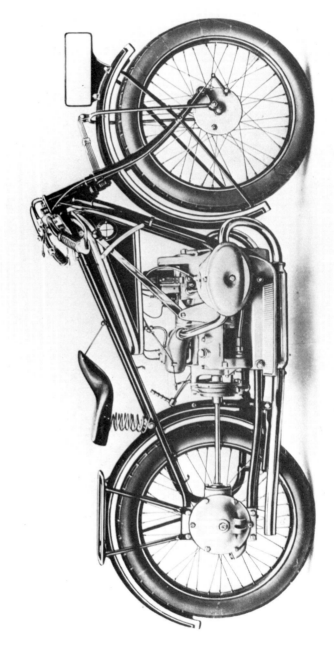

R47

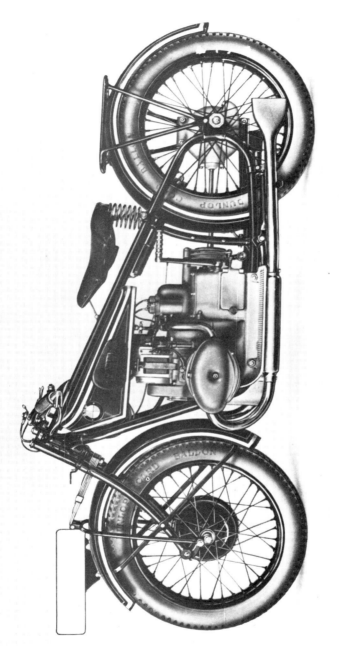

R57

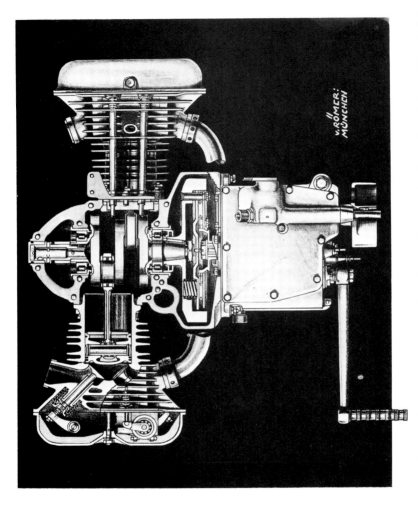

Revealed in the R57 engine are rolling-element bearings for the rocker shafts and for the big-ends; concealed is the built-up construction of the crankshaft, necessary for the one-piece conrods.

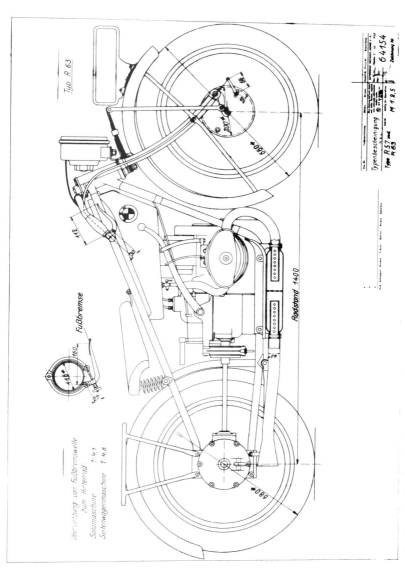

The footbrake detailed on the R57/63 drawing is the same as that on the R42, but the front brake is much bigger: 200mm was very generous in the late 1920s.

R63

R62

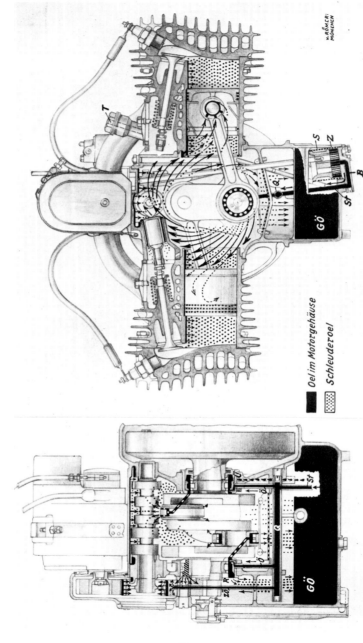

BMW artists were still not giving away all the details of crankshaft build even in this R11 engine, but the two-tier cooling of the detachable heads was interesting.

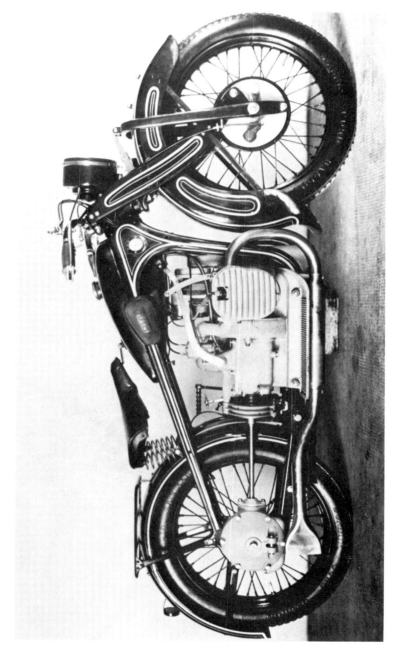

The Star frame of the R11 should have made pressed steel more popular in motorcycles than it did.

R16 series 4, 1933

CHAPTER 2

JOY THROUGH STRENGTH

Designing motorcycles is a risky business, in which the most important consideration affecting the decision-making processes is an extreme commercial caution. Any departure from the norms that have become accepted by the customers will be met with a curiosity founded on suspicion. Any change in design concepts amounting to revolution or even accelerated evolution will be welcomed as a talking point in the media where acolytes discuss their faith; but because their faith is based on received dogma, that welcome is unlikely to be extended to the market place. The traditional motorcyclist is extremely conservative, if only because his resources—whether material or educational—are too limited to allow him the luxury of taking radical or reformatory risks. There is a way for the designer to break out of this rut, and this is to seek markets where the traditional customer does not exist. Seldom is this possible: it happened in the 1950s in Europe with the phenomenal success of the motor scooter (a success that was ephemeral for reasons extraneous to the industry and to this argument), it happened in the USA in the 1960s when new Japanese manufacturers introduced novel engineering concepts to an untapped and unprejudiced market, and it could happen again in the latter 1970s. The fact that BMW did not seek to make it happen in Germany in the late 1930s is one that may or may not be lamented but should be remarked.

At that time, German industry was exulting in an orgy of technological advance. It may have been due to opportunism or to optimism; it may have been in order to represent the beneficial consequences of adopting the national socialist ideology, or to misrepresent them; but whatever the reason, laudable or deplorable, enormous progress was being made. It was an industrial revelation in which the German engineers saw a new heaven and a new earth because the old heaven and the old earth had passed away—for better or worse, an afterthought that St. John of Ephesus omitted from his earlier apocalypse. The engineers of BMW were active participants: they were leading the race for a viable gas turbine aero-engine, and they were putting the finishing touches to the world's first modern sports car. Why, seeing that they were the leaders of the German motorcycle industry, were they not equally adventurous in that field?

They probably thought they were. In view of the priorities imposed by governmental policy and by their own financial comptrollers' desire for profit, it is unlikely that more than a tiny proportion of their highest quality brain-hours was devoted to the motorcycles. Furthermore they were already conscious of having a tradition to maintain, and in a country brought up for centuries to take a pride in local craftsmanship and local schools of design, tradition died hard. In the case of the BMW motorcycle, the essential elements of the tradition were quite clear, comprising a transverse flat-twin engine with its clutch, gearbox and shaft drive ranged more or less in line astern to arrive at an enclosed bevel-gear final drive for the rear wheel nestling in the extremities of a double loop frame. Virtually all these components were mutually interdependent, for the layout consti-tuted a completely logical entity: to alter any part of it would equally logically demand alteration of the whole. There was no good reason for doing so: it was pretty good as it stood. Certainly it was not perfect; but if criticism was easy, it was because all motorcycles then and since have been conspicuously far from perfection, and all BMWs by the standards of their time have been (equally conspicuously) less susceptible of criticism than most of their contemporaries. There are grounds for harping over the basic layout of the BMW, according to one's preferred resolution of the arguments that turn on such matters as torque reaction, gyroscopic precession, drive-line inertia, the distribution of forces applied through the final drive, and the penalties of increased frontal area and limited angle of bank. In the 1920s and even in the 1930s such objections were literally of no great moment: rates of crankshaft revolution were low, as was fuel quality, and these two factors combined to ensure that engine power was modest and flexibility considerable. These machines would pull well from very low speeds in top gear, and people simply did not change gear as much as they do today. As for fears of grounding a cylinder head, neither the tyres nor the road surfaces were conducive to high coefficients of friction, so it followed that cornering rates and corresponding angles of banks were commensurately modest— say 0.85g and 40 degrees as a normal maximum. Take into account the rigid rear wheel location and the limited deflexion of the front suspension, so that ground clearance would not be diminished by bump loading, and it becomes clear that none of the theoretical objections to the BMW layout amounted to much in practice.

If anything needed to be changed, it was the cycle rather than the motor. As Henne's supercharged 750 had confirmed often enough, the BMW was capable of going amply fast in a straight line; but any line of less rectitude might involve some alarming changes of attitude, as the steering and suspension fought for supremacy and the rider fought for control. Those bottom-link forks were too compliant, and the springing not pliant enough, and the need to produce something better had been exercising the appropriate minds of Munich for some time. In 1935 we saw the outcome of their studies, when the R12 and R17 appeared with telescopic front forks.

They were not by any means the first telescopics to feature in a motorcycle, various attempts to produce something generically similar dating back as many as thirty years. They were however the first telescopic forks that (especially after another forty years) could be deemed recognizably modern, the first such to incorporate hydraulic dampers in a series-production motorcycle. Compared with the old trailing bottom-link arrangement with its multiplicity of small bushes and large leverages, the new forks were practically maintenance-free and had an incomparably longer life, as well as being much less liable to distortion. They also had a much longer spring travel: in those days an axial compression of 88 mm was really thought very generous, even though it corresponded to appreciably less wheel movement in terms of vertical displacement, such was the rake of the forks. Most other protagonists of telescopic forks took it for granted, if only for manufacturing convenience, that the fork stanchions should be parallel to the steering head; but BMW realised early that, by having the stanchions raked further away from the vertical than the steering head, it would be possible to minimise the variation of steering trail that accompanied pitching oscillation—one of the drawbacks of telescopic forks and a destabilising influence that is still apparent on many of today's motorcycles. Doubtless their enquiries into this aspect of suspension and steering interaction had been prompted by an analysis of the behaviour of their earlier bottom-link suspension, in which such variations were implicit though minimised by the good old-fashioned system of minimising spring deflexion and wheel travel.

It may be that in fact the most important contribution to the new-found excellence of ride and steering was due not to the geometry of BMW's telescopic forks but to the suitability and sensitivity of the integral hydraulic dampers which were so much better fitted for their task than the friction dampers on which the rest of the motor-cycling world rode. Be that as it may, the R12 and R17 earned praise for their straight-line stability and generally better steering, as well as for the much improved durability that the new fork construction promised.

Nor were these the only distinctions of the new models. They were powerful: the R17 in particular was the lustiest motorcycle BMW had yet produced, developing 33 horsepower at 4500 rpm, which was correspondingly the highest crankshaft rate of any up to that time. It followed that the R17 was the fastest BMW yet, with a maximum speed of 140 km/h (87 mph). It was but little heavier than the R11, yet despite the greater reserve of power it shared with the more modestly endowed R12 a new four-speed gearbox, still with a gate-type gearchange built into the knee pad. There were minor changes too, including the removal of the speedometer from the petrol tank to the headlamp shell where it was easier to see; but most interesting of these minor refinements was the fact that for the first time the front and rear wheels of the motorcycle were interchangeable.

After what had been some years of stagnation, these improvements, while welcome, might have seemed less than might have been expected.

Anyone hoping for more could well have been satisfied the following year when a BMW that was almost completely new came on the market. The pride of 1936 was the R5, with a substantially new 500 cc engine rendering 24 bhp and doing it at an unprecedented 5800 rpm. To make such rates possible, the pushrods of the overhead-valve engine had to be made as short and light as could be, and this was achieved by duplicating the camshafts, which were driven by a timing chain running a triangular course. The superiority of hairpin valve springs, which were virtually immune from the bounce and surge that affects the helical variety, had been proved in racing and was now exploited in this road machine, which was distinguished by rocker boxes of a new shape. It could as readily be distinguished by its frame, for with this model BMW returned again to the closed triangular double loop tubes. It was no longer of brazed construction as in the past, but exploited new electrical welding techniques. More intriguing still, the tubes were not of constant section but were in some cases of conical elliptical form to secure a very high bending moment in the chosen plane. With the increased structural stiffness thus conferred, it became feasible to increase the spring travel in the front forks to more than 100 mm, a change that was accompanied by the provision of adjustment for the hydraulic damping. There was only one loss to be mourned, for the traditional cast aluminium alloy footboards had gone, to be replaced by common footpegs, while the old heel-operated rear brake pedal gave way to a more modern toe brake. Perhaps it was the demands of the new pedal arrangements that prompted the abolition of those lovely old foot-boards, for the two-shaft gearbox of the R5 had a foot-operated gearlever. At the time such a device was not considered completely reliable, so a tiny hand lever was provided as well.

The conservatism that demanded such a belt-and-braces approach demanded also a plonkworthy side-valver for those duties where the sporting ohv R5 might be feared too intransigent. It got it in the R6, which appeared the following year and set a new BMW standard by offering an engine of 600 cc displacement, instead of the nominal 750 of tradition. There had been a clue to this in October 1936, when Henne raised the world speed record for motorcycles to

272 km/h (169 mph)—a much bigger increment than usual in commercialised record-breaking—with a new 500 cc streamliner. The wonders he had done with the big 750 faded in comparison with what this dramatic aerodyne achieved, for the whole machine and rider were enclosed in an ovoid aluminium shell with a tail fin; but a week before the record-shattering run took place on the Frankfurt-Darmstadt Autobahn, team manager Schleicher had said *We are finished with the 750—the blown 500 is already giving much more power.* So it must have been, for there were rumours of an unofficial clocking of the flying egg at something like 200 mph during 6 am practice runs on the more sinuous Autobahn running from Munich to Landengränze. Eric Fernihough, who had taken his Brough Superior to the same venue, had no hope of competing, and it was only six months later that his 1000 cc V-twin proved able to better Henne's speed, and then only by 1 km/h. BMW professed to take no notice, but when after a further six months the Italians had the temerity to push the record up again, albeit by an even tinier margin, with a 500 cc Gilera in the capable hands of Piero Taruffi, their response was almost immediate. Within five weeks Henne had the BMW 500 out on the Frankfurt-Munich Autobahn, where he lifted the world record to 279.5 km/h (173.7 mph), there to remain undisturbed for fourteen years.

Like the Gilera, the BMW 500 record-breaker was supercharged. So had been the 750 since 1929, when the basic R63 had been modified with a positive-displacement blower bolted on top of the gearbox and driven by the magneto shaft, its location providing quite convenient runs for the pipes carrying the charge to the cylinders. The record-breaking 500, however, followed the pattern of the similar-sized racers, with the supercharger (the final choice was the most effective of the eccentric vane varieties, the Zoller) built on to the front of the crankcase, whence long induction pipes went snaking underneath the cylinders to reach the rearward-facing cylinder-head ports.

The superiority and power of the factory's blown 500 cc racers was made more emphatic in 1935 with the introduction of a new racing engine featuring a barrel-type crankcase from the top of which a single tube emerged above each cylinder to carry a shaft driving twin overhead camshafts. Apart from the crankcase and the valve springs, this machine also gave a foretaste of the R5 in being fitted with hydraulically damped telescopic front forks; but although this last feature was a complete novelty in racing, it was still no more than a half-hearted attempt to match the roadholding proclivities of the factory's sternest British and Italian rivals. From the earliest days of motorcycling, there had been spasmodic experiments with the fully sprung frame, including most notably the elegant suspension of the ABC that appeared to have so much to do with the inspiration of Max Friz; but it was in the mid-1930s, when racing motorcycles had already as much power as they could use, that it began to demand proper attention. The eminently successful Guzzi of 1935 had demonstrated the virtues of the spring-heeled bicycle fairly effectively; but it was when Freddie Frith handed his Norton to a marshal after winning the 1936 Junior TT and ran, actually *ran,* up the paddock, that the era of the spring-framed motorcycle was confirmed in its arrival. Such a display would have been unthinkable in earlier years, because the spine-jarring ride of the rigid-frame motorcycle left the rider shattered and exhausted after completing the punishing course. The Nortons for 1936 had spring frames, however, and this not only improved the already outstanding roadholding of the Norton but also gave a more comfortable ride, as Frith so vividly demonstrated. The Norton rear suspension was of the plunger type, that prompted wags to refer to its frame as the 'garden gate'; but Velocette also turned up in that year with spring frames of remarkably modern conception, combining a trailing fork with telescopic suspension units in which compressed air provided the springing medium and oil the damping. The Vincent HRD, by this time the uncrowned king of Britain's and the world's roadburners, had long made the most of a sprung rear wheel, and one of the ways it exploited its superior adhesion was in very efficient braking given by twin drums on each wheel, arranged to produce a symmetry of braking forces which avoided the distortion that might otherwise take place in the front forks. Germany's lightweight DKW racer had even bigger brakes (and being a two-stroke it needed them) disposed centrally in the wheel to produce some of the same freedom from distortion, a consideration that BMW might have been well advised to examine in view of the poor resistance of telescopic forks to distortion thus induced.

It must be admitted that, despite their technological leadership, the German and Italian firms that rejoiced in the patronage of their totalitarian masters were not yet able to topple the old-fashioned but thoroughly developed British factory racers from their familiar pinnacle in top-flight international racing. Despite their lack of power, the 350 and 500 Nortons of 1936 could make the best possible use of such power as they had, and won every big race but one. Nevertheless, by the end of that year the British riders were complaining that no unsupercharged single-cylinder machine (as theirs were) could compare for speed and acceleration with the supercharged BMW. They could not hope for much longer to rely on the superior road-holding of their new spring-framed bicycles, for by the end of 1936 the racing BMW was similarly sprung.

It was surprisingly soon afterwards that the same improvement was made to BMW production motorcycles. In 1938 their springing was introduced at the rear of the new 500 cc R51, with the necessary adjunct of a universally jointed drive shaft. In other respects the R51, and its prodigious 30 bhp big brother the 600 cc R66, were largely the same as the R5, while the side-valve R61 of 600 cc and R71 of 750 cc followed the same pattern with such modifications as were appropriate to sidecar duty.

This adoption of full springing across the board was well enough justified by the success of the spring-heeled racers. No longer were BMW content to limit their campaigning to the continental circus: in 1937 they extended their threat to British supremacy by forays into the Isle of Man and Northern Ireland. It takes more than technical superiority to win in the Isle of Man, it takes familiarity with the exceptional demands of that incomparable circuit: so it was by no means a disgraceful Manx debut for BMW when Jock West finished the 1937 Senior T T in sixth place. When he went on to win the Ulster Grand Prix, there were few doubts left about the ability of the BMW. The Bavarian team might have been expected to make a rather better showing in the following year, but things went wrong.

Old-timer Karl Gall, number three rider of the works team, was injured in practice. Georg Meier (who was to end the year as European champion) was eliminated on the starting line when a hasty change from the soft warming-up spark plugs to the hard racing ones resulted in a stripped thread in one of the aluminium cylinder heads. That just left Jock West, who seems from the evidence to have ridden at his personal limit to put the remaining BMW into fifth place on the results list. The British were still at the top.

The same three riders represented BMW in the Island in 1939. Their motorcycles did not look significantly different from those of the previous year; many of their opponents looked quite different, and that may have been quite significant. In fact the BMWs were truly new machines: a neat little identification plate on the front forks confirmed the year of manufacture as 1939, as well as the engine displacement of 494 cc. Those sections of the panel dealing with power output and weight were left tactfully empty, but of course those figures were the most significant of all.

The true power output of the supercharged 500 cc BMW racer in its final form has never been revealed. Estimates have ranged from 50 bhp, which is a ludicrous mistake, probably arising from confusion with the post-war unblown racer, to 105 which is as improbable as the lower figure was inadequate. Of all the intervening estimates, the most convincing is the figure of 68 bhp, for it corresponds to a peak-power brake mean effective pressure of about 15 atmospheres: bearing in mind the state of the art in Germany in the latter 1930s, when (before their adoption of two-stage supercharging) the racing car manufacturers were achieving slightly higher pressures with similar boost but with the advantages of liquid cooling to offset the disadvantages of larger cylinders, such a level of volumetric efficiency seems about right.

However vague we may be about the power of the blown BMW, there is no doubt about its weight. After the completion of scrutineering for the Senior T T field in 1939, the ACU published the weights of all competing machines. The BMW was the lightest of the lot, the works machines turning the scales at a mere 306 lb, which makes an interesting comparison with the standard over-the-counter racing BMW at 351 lb and the production R51 at 400. The British racers in the Senior class were all in the region of 330 lb, the 350s for the Junior being only 15 lb lighter. There were some surprises in the lightweight class, for despite the traditional name for the 250s they included a Benelli that seemed surprisingly hefty at 293 lb, compared with the 238 of the rival Rudge, though modest compared with the 250 DKW which weighed 320 lb, 16 less than its 350 cc stablemate. One of the heaviest motorcycles running was the Junior NSU whose net 369 lb weight was supplemented by 50 lb of fuel to cater for its terribly heavy fuel consumption; the V4 AJS 500, water-cooled, supercharged, four-cylindered and girder-forked, also had a dipsomaniac thirst and a fuel tank to match, and its basic weight was 405 lb. Small wonder that it could not compete with the BMW.

Neither could anything else. It seemed at first as though the team were to be doomed to the same sort of bad luck as had dogged them in 1938. This time the tragedy was greater: Karl Gall, who had been a stalwart since the earliest days of BMW racing, and had been German road racing champion in 1937, was killed in the first day's practice. However, when race day came, practice had made it clear to Meier and West that their machines were comfortably superior to everything else in the event. Meier won the Senior TT in 1939 at a record race speed of 89.38 mph, with such apparent ease that there was no need for him to exceed the lap record speed of 91 mph that had formed part of Harold Daniell's winning Norton ride a year earlier. West finished second.

It was the first time since 1911 that the Senior category of this great British race had been won by foreigners. Nor was it only in road racing that the British and BMW were at loggerheads: ever since that first courageous foray by Rudolf Schleicher into the International Six Days Trial, BMW motorcycles had featured increasingly often in this most rigorous and respected event of the roughriders' calendar. In 1935, indeed, the German team rode *supercharged* 500 cc BMWs with telescopic front forks! It was rumoured that the German Trophy team members could expect to share a bonus of £600 (perhaps the equivalent of £9,000 today?) if they won . . . as in fact they did. In later years they were even more highly organised, enjoying the patronage, if that was the word, of Korpsführer Huhnlein, the Nazi leader of organised sport. In 1937 the German Trophy team on BMWs lost to the British in a fast and furious event, staged mostly in Wales, by the slender margin of 10 seconds after nearly a thousand miles of very hard going. As for the Vase section of the event, this was marred by the discovery of a mistake in the timekeeping which led to the German Army team having its first place taken away from it and given to the Dutch—but since both those teams rode BMWs, the factory was presumably not upset too much by the decision. In 1938 it was the German A team on 500 cc BMWs that won the Vase while Britain won the Trophy, but in the following year events were rather less happy. War hung in the air, and an argument about fuel supplies, failure to resolve which would have put the British out of the running, ended not in formal protest but in the British team simply packing up and going home. The event took place in the vicinity of Salzburg, and since everybody realised that war might be declared at any moment, the Germans had given their assurance that if that were to happen the foreign competitors would be allowed to leave. They were as good as their word: far from obstructing the flight of the British riders, they assisted in every way they could. Motorcycling sport has always been pretty healthy (if not very sanitary!), but competition of this particular sort between BMW and their arch-rivals from Britain would have to go into abeyance for long years to come. As 1939 wore on to its distracted end, the demands of war stopped the production of BMW motorcycles for civilian use. They had had a good run, more than a hundred and sixty thousand having been built since the first R32 sixteen years earlier had put the company on its feet. BMW were now very firmly on their feet: the 1938 figures of 180 million Marks turnover and 18,624 people on the payroll had shattered all their previous records, but 1939 saw a turnover lifted to 275 million, employees to 26,919, and the reserves (that the company had once been quite happy to keep level at about 400,000 Marks) now stood at 54 million. It was not all due to motorcycles, not by any means, but without the motorcycles there would have been nothing. And after all, motorcycle production was not being stopped completely: for military purposes it was to continue—but the Army wanted something better than the simple single-cylinder BMW it had once been content to buy.

	R12	R17	R5
ENGINE Type Number	M56 S6	M60 S4	254/1
Cylinders, bore, stroke mm	2x78x78	2x83x68	2x68x68
Displacement cm^3	745	734	494
Compression ratio :1	5.2	6.5	6.7
Valve location	s	oh	oh
Camshaft(s)			2
Carburettor(s)	1 Sum	2 Amal	2 Amal
Power PS max	18	33	24
at rev/min	3400	5000	5800
Corresponding bmep kg/cm^2	6.49	8.21	7.65
Oil, capacity, litres	2	2.5	2
TRANSMISSION Type Number	212/1	G212/1a	250/1
Gear ratios :1 i	2.92	2.92	2.77
top gear ii	1.89	1.89	1.75
iii	1.30	1.30	1.31
iv	1	1	1
Final drive ratio :1	4.07 or 4.75	4.07 or 4.75	3.89 or 4.62
CHASSIS Type Number	212/1	212/1	250/1
Frame	pressed steel	pressed steel	tubular cradle
Front forks	telescopic	telescopic	telescopic
springing	internal helical	internal helical	internal helical
damping	hydraulic	hydraulic	hydraulic
Rear forks	unsprung	unsprung	unsprung
Front brake type	drum 1LS	drum 1LS	drum 1LS
diameter mm	200	200	200
Rear brake type	drum 1LS	drum 1LS	drum 1LS
Tyres	3.5x19	3.5x19	3.5x19
Fuel tank, litres	14	14	15
Weight, kg	185	183	165
Maximum speed km/h	110	140	135-140
Frame numbers	P501-24728*	P501-24728	8001-9504 (1936)*
Engine numbers	501-24149**	77001-77436	8001-9504 (1936)‡
Quantity built	36000	450	2600
Years of Production	1935–8	1935–7	1936–7

* and 25101-37161

** and 25001-37161

*500001-503085 in 1937

‡ 500001-502586 in 1937

	R6	R51	R61
ENGINE Type Number	261/1	254/1	261/1
Cylinders, bore, stroke mm	2x70x78	2x68x68	2x70x78
Displacement cm^3	600	494	600
Compression ratio :1	6	6.7	5.7
Valve location	s	oh	s
Camshaft(s)	2	2	2
Carburettor(s)	2 Amal	2 Amal or Bing	2 Amal or Bing
Power PS max	18	24	18
at rev/min	4800	5600	4800
Corresponding bmep kg/cm^2	5.71	7.92	5.71
Oil capacity, litres	2	2	2
TRANSMISSION Type Number	250/1	250/2	250/2
Gear ratios :1 i	2.77	2.77	2.77
top gear ii	1.75	1.75	1.75
iii	1.31	1.31	1.31
iv	1	1	1
Final drive ratio :1	3.89 or 4.62	3.89 or 4.62	3.89 or 4.62
CHASSIS Type Number	250/1	251/1	251/1
Frame	tubular cradle	tubular cradle	tubular cradle
Front forks	telescopic	telescopic	telescopic
springing	internal helical	internal helical	internal helical
damping	hydraulic	hydraulic	hydraulic
Rear forks	unsprung	plunger	plunger
springing		internal helical	internal helical
damping		none	none
Front brake type	drum 1LS	drum 1LS	drum 1LS
diameter mm	200	200	200
Rear brake type	drum 1LS	drum 1LS	drum 1LS
Tyres	3.5x19	3.5x19	3.5x19
Fuel tank, litres	15	14	14
Weight, kg	175	182	184
Maximum speed km/h	125	135-140	110-115
Frame numbers	500001-503085	505001-515164	*
Engine numbers	600001-601850	503001-506172	603001-606080*
Quantity built	1850	13000	13000
Years of production	1937	1938—40	1938—41

* 607001-607340 in 1941

	R66	R71
ENGINE Type Number	266/1	271/1
Cylinders, bore, stroke mm	2x69.8x78	2x78x78
Displacement cm^3	597	745
Compression ratio :1	6.8	5.5
Valve location	oh	s
Camshaft(s)	2	2
Carburettor(s)	2 Amal or Bing	2 Graetzin
Power PS max	30	22
at rev/min	5300	4600
Corresponding bmep kg/cm^2	8.65	5.86
Oil capacity, litres	2	2
TRANSMISSION Type Number	250/2	250/2
Gear ratios :1 i	2.77	2.77
top gear ii	1.75	1.75
iii	1.31	1.31
iv	1	1
Final drive ratio :1	3.6 or 4.38	3.6 or 3.89
CHASSIS Type number	251/1	251/1
Frame	tubular cradle	tubular cradle
Front forks	telescopic	telescopic
springing	internal helical	internal helical
damping	hydraulic	hydraulic
Rear forks	plunger	plunger
springing	internal helical	internal helical
damping	none	none
Front brake type	drum 1LS	drum 1LS
diameter mm	200	200
Rear brake type	drum 1LS	drum 1LS
Tyres	3.5x19	3.5x19
Fuel tank, litres	14	14
Weight, kg	187	187
Maximum speed km/h	145	125
Frame numbers	505001-515164	505001-515164*
Engine numbers	662001-662039	700001-702200*
Quantity built	2000	2000
Years of production	1938—41	1938—41

*703001-703511 in 1941

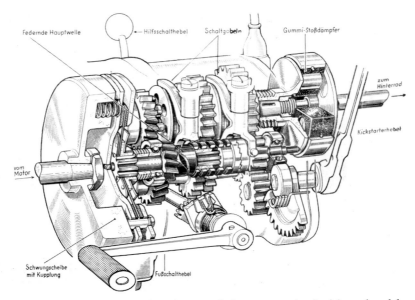

Belt and braces: the novel footchange of the R5 was backed by a hand lever.

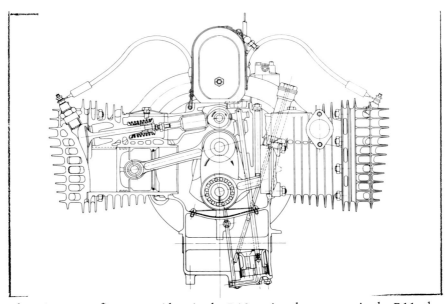

There is more refinement evident in the R12 engine than we saw in the R11; the centre throw of the crankshaft is now elliptical.

Twin-carburettor version of the R12.

Single-carburettor R12 in utility finish.

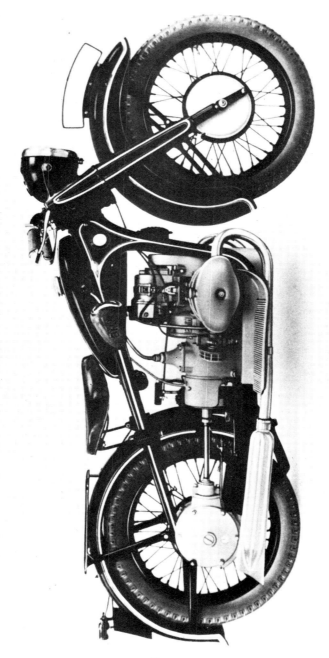

R17

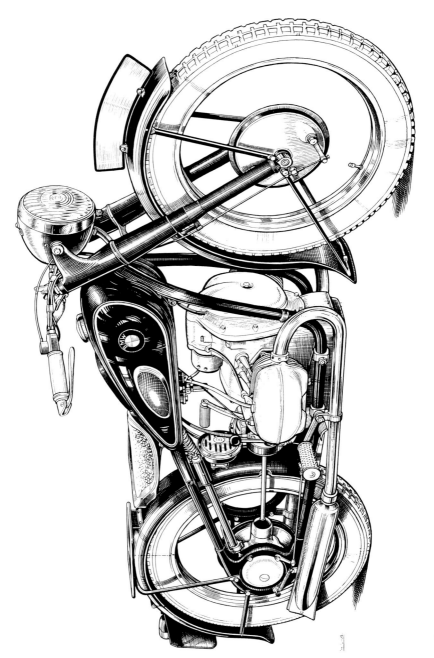

R.5

R 5

R6

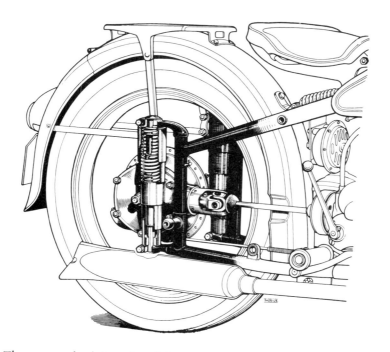

The sprung heel introduced in 1938: note the sidecar-fixing lug.

R51

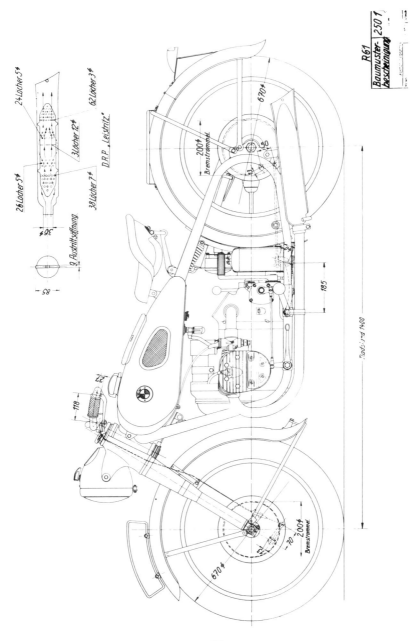

The drawing proclaims the R61, but in error, this is the R6.

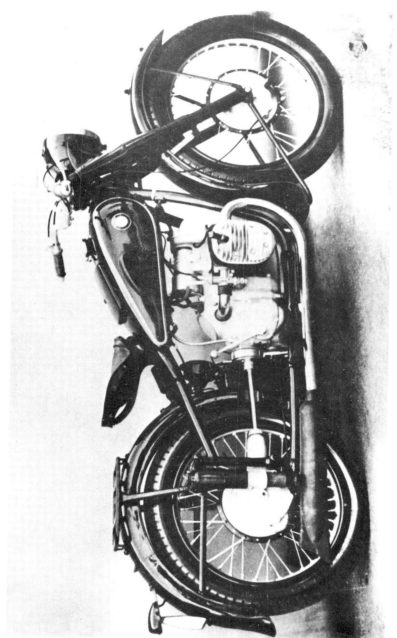

R61

R60

R71 with sidecar in army camouflage.

Somebody had a wicked sense of fun when shaping this dummy rider with long super-penetrant nose for the Stuttgart wind-tunnel experiments conducted on the supercharged racer. The cowling in front of the steering head was quite effective (of the R90S!) in reducing drag. A tiny detail, worthy of note on this presumably temperamental racer, was the plug spanner carried ready above the gearbox.

CHAPTER 3

BABY GRAND

A two-cylinder engine, if its cylinders and their respective crankpins be alike disposed at 180 degree intervals about a common crankshaft (and if the axes of those cylinders are as little offset as is compatible with the need for the overlap of the connecting rods) may be made just about as perfectly balanced and free from vibrations as it is possible for a two-cylinder engine with a single crankshaft and finite-length connecting rods to be. Doubling the number of cylinders will not make its balance any better, but halving that number will wreck it. There is no way of making a single-cylinder engine perfectly balanced; yet BMW, who embarked on motorcycle manufacture in such a style as to suggest that fully balanced flat twins were a fundamental tenet of their faith, went on to make motorcycles with single-cylinder engines, and made them in large numbers.

The single-cylinder engine may be worse than the flat twin or indeed any other. It is also cheaper and simpler, and there can always be found people who would rather have something imperfect than have nothing at all. When BMW demeaned themselves to make single-cylinder machines, they did it for just such people: when they embarked on a two-year run of the R39 in 1925, and more particularly when they put the R2 into production in 1931, they did so because they had to, rather than because they wanted to. There are times when ideals can be like millstones.

Yet there were some ideals that BMW never abandoned. In an earlier chapter the point was made that the seminal Friz concept of the R32 was an organic entity, incapable of alteration in any of its essentials without altering its entire character. It would be easy to surmise that the whole system of engine and transmission grew out of the attractions of the horizontally opposed two-cylinder engine, if only because that preceded the entire motorcycle in production at Munich. The lawyers have an axiom, *qui prior est tempore potior est jure*—but bad law makes hard cases. The fact that BMW could allow themselves to make single-cylinder engines makes clear what were the priorities of their faith, which never allowed them to sacrifice the shaft-drive transmission. Indeed it would be quite wrong to accuse them of having prostituted their talents in producing the singles as a commercial expedient: it seemed to them right, and was early made into a firm policy yet to be transgressed, (though transgression is anticipated by 1979) that any motorcycle with an engine capacity smaller than the 500 cc class (which, the conventions of motorcycle classification being what they have so long been, meant 400 cc or less) ought to have but one cylinder.

The first of these was a 250 cc lightweight, the R39, which appeared only two years after the sensational R32 twin. The engine of the 500 cc twin was, it will be remembered, an uprated modified version of the one that had formerly been incorporated longitudinally in the Helios: in the R32 it developed 8.5 bhp—but such was progress in the 1920s that the R39, with just half its cylindrical endowment, developed as much power as the original Douglas-inspired engine for the Helios, and the little 250 cc motorcycle was actually faster than the 500 twin from which it was derived.

In some ways it was also more elegant. According to Dr Helmut Bönsch, it was the first motorcycle engine in the world to have fully enclosed overhead valve mechanism. It must be remembered that the 1920s was a period when many vehicle designers were inspired by an aesthetic sensibility so acute in some instances that they allowed their artistic notions to get the better of their engineering principles and degenerated into being mere stylists. It was fashionable for motor car engineers to require an engine to appear as nearly as possible monolithic, uncluttered by ancillaries, auxiliaries, or even the basic manifolding necessary for tolerable volumetric efficiency: Bugatti, Voisin, Roesch, and many others, pursued this chimaera with varying degrees of success, either commercial or aesthetic. Some small efforts were sporadically made to do the same thing in motorcycles, but the very nature of the machines made it virtually impossible, and only in the simplest principles did the engine of the R39 BMW espouse this curious and short-lived cause. It was the better for it, because after discarding all the quasi-artistic fancies associated with the fashion, what was left was a nice piece of clean, practical and durable engineering: the cylinder and crankcase were cast in one piece from aluminium alloy, the iron cylinder sleeve being thereafter pressed into position.

Was this really a poor man's motorcycle? With a price ticket of 1870 Marks, it did not seem very much cheaper than the 2200-Mark R32; but that was hardly a fair comparison, bearing in mind how inflation was raging in the 1920s. Two years could make an awful lot of difference, and it was fair to compare the R39 with its strictly contemporary and in most details identical stablemate the 2900-Mark R37. On that basis the R39 was quite surprisingly cheap.

Maybe this relatively low price revealed a much smaller profit margin than for the R37 twin. If that were so and the R39 was intended as a kind of loss-leader, then the plan backfired; for the little single enjoyed sufficient demand to keep it in production for a thousand examples, whereas the R37 got no further than 175—but for that matter the R37 got no further than the year 1926, when the better-developed R42 twin came along and ran to 6900 examples in its turn. By the end of 1927, with the R42 also in production and the sporting R47 on the stocks, there was no longer any need for BMW to trouble themselves with the relatively less profitable lightweight single, and they abandoned it.

Little did they know what was coming. Yet when finally the slump did hit hard, they had had some premonition of potential disaster and were able to start work soon enough on their 'people's motor-cycle', the feebly utilitarian R2. This appeared in 1931, which will be remembered as in the days of the pressed-steel Star frame, a contraption which for all its intriguing lightness and stiffness looked surprisingly bulky. Within its generous embrace the little 200 cc engine of the R2 seemed almost lost, especially if one were looking at it from the left of the bicycle; but this was because the whole engine was offset to the right side of the centre line so that direct drive might be possible in top gear all the way from the crankshaft to the final drive. When you only have 6 bhp at your disposal, and your ambitions extend to a giddy 85 km/h (53 mph), you simply cannot afford the power losses of any unnecessary multiplicity of gears: a three-shaft double-reduction gearbox (or at least an all-indirect two-shaft box) was necessary for the twins because their crankshafts had to be disposed along the centre lines of their frames, and the drive had to be stepped out to the axis of the propeller shaft. With the single-cylinder engines these constraints did not apply: one can imagine the designers being tempted with the idea of setting the single cylinder horizontal with its head towards the left and its crankcase out on the right aligned with the drive shaft.

Evidently it was not necessary and presumably the people (the plebeian customers for the *Volksmotorrad*) would not have understood. Their misgivings were to be allayed at almost any price, even at the market price of 975 Marks. It must have worked, for in five or six years BMW sold more than 15,000 of the things. They were helped even more by the agreement of the army to buy a more powerful version, the 400 cc R4, in 1932. This was made available to the public as well, was produced in almost exactly equal quantity, and by the standards of its time probably seemed quite spritely, being capable of 100 km/h (62 mph), having 12 bhp at its disposal and weighing but a quarter more than its half-sized sibling.

By the time it appeared, the R2 had grown a little less lethargic, its power output having been raised from 6 to 8 bhp. It put on a little weight, too, despite the advent of a light alloy cylinder head, but was still not as heavy as the sheet steel pressings made it look. To reduce their apparent bulk, lots of elegant white lining had to be applied by hand, as always, on critical areas of its glossy black enamel, producing a high-quality appearance that was somehow curiously at odds with the machine's utilitarian purposes. That is marketing for you: the customer is always happiest to pay for what he sees.

In the economy sector of the market, he is reluctant to pay for something that seems in any way strange. The people who bought the big twin accepted as part of the BMW mystique the kick-starter located on the left of the machine and swinging out in a plane perpendicular to the drive line. On the R2 and R4 the kick-starter was on the right. By 1934 the kick-starter of the R4 had been geared so that it swung in an arc, just like that of any common conventional motorcycle with a transverse crankshaft, a change which had the virtue of making the kick-starter easier to operate while astride the machine. By this time (it was done in 1933) the decision had been taken that all single-cylinder BMWs should have peg-type pedals instead of footboards, making the use of the geared kick-starter less hazardous to the shins.

There were other oddities in these curious machines. The R2 and earlier versions of the R4 had a simple rigid direct-acting car-type gearlever sprouting from the top of the gearbox and slanting up and forwards alongside the cylinder. In 1935 the R4 was uprated to 14 bhp, and now that it was more mettlesome it was treated to a rubber shock-absorber in the drive line; and then in 1936 it was time for it to be joined by a 300 cc version, the R3, again with its engine offset to permit a direct-drive top gear. It all seemed to be making for an excessive elaboration of the range; and when telescopic forks were handed down from the big twins to the singles in 1937, a happy compromise was achieved with a single engine size of 350 cc, offering the same 14 bhp as the R4 at higher rpm (the stroke was the same) and not unreasonably reaching the same 100 km/h top speed. Anybody fondly supposing that the advent of telescopic forks would allow the 350 single to be ridden hard with the same security and comfort as on the big twins was in for a rude awakening: the front forks of the R35 were devoid of damping. BMW must have studied their customers closely and learned that in this particular market they would not pay good Marks for funny oil-filled contraptions that they could neither see nor understand.

In fact the single-cylinder range grew steadily more cynical in its specification. 1937 and 38 saw the addition to the range of the 190 cc R20 and the 250 cc R23, still with undamped telescopic forks, but now with welded tubular frames that made them look lighter than the original R2 and R4 though in fact they were heavier. The four-speed gearbox of the R35 was evidently judged an extravagance in this context, so the newcomers reverted to three-speeders, albeit with foot-operated change. There must have been consolation for somebody in the disposition of the kick-starter pedal, though; it had moved back to its proper BMW disposition on the left of the machine, swinging outwards. It was less convenient, but the inconvenience did not matter because the machines were so slow that the time lost was immaterial. It may have been more important that customers felt as though they had something like a real BMW—that is, one of the twins—and some such brand loyalty or self-deception must have been responsible for the quite healthy sales of these pre-war singles. Thirteen thousand people must have loved them, however briefly, but at least serving soldiers were spared the burden that so many civilians voluntarily undertook: after the R4, the army lost interest in singles. The army had other, more substantial, matters to occupy it; and eleven eventful years were to pass between the cessation of manufacture of the pre-war singles in 1938 and the revival of the R24 single which was the first BMW motorcycle to be built after the war.

Things could so easily have been different. When in 1948 BMW were given permission to build motorcycles not exceeding 250 cc displacement they had a very interesting lightweight machine on the stocks. It had been developed in secret, and although it was a two-stroke it was much more like a genuine miniature BMW whereas all the previous pseudo-lightweights were more like a standard double-breasted tourer that had suffered some kind of Amazonian mastectomy. The prototype was a horizontally-opposed twin with shaft drive, in other words; its displacement was only 125 cc, but in the BMW context that was no more a traduction of tradition than the fact that it was a two-stroke. It had a lot of good features that made it a promising design—but it did not go into production. Considering the fate of the promising and convention-defying new machines that were going into production in other countries, only to wither and die in the blighting miasma of customer conservatism, it was probably just as well. Instead, BMW came back with the mixture as before: the R24 was a development of the pre-war singles but better looking and with a less crabbed specification. The engine was particularly clean externally and more powerful than any previous BMW of similar capacity, not that that was saying a lot. Some of the details were more interesting, such as the new Noris dynamo (actually by Bosch), the automatic ignition advance, and the four-speed gearbox in which the shock absorber was a spring-loaded face cam instead of the rubber coupling of the pre-war utility. There was still a rather utilitarian look about the R24 though, with its bolted-up frame and that little auxiliary hand-lever for the gearchange that always makes one wonder what on earth is wrong with the pedal linkage.

The extra lever was still there on the R25 of 1950, but this was a much better-turned-out machine. The new tubular frame incorporated the plunger rear suspension that also figured in the twins which were allowed into production that same year, and like them it featured such niceties as interchangeable wheels and straight-ended spokes. The power output was supposed to be the same as that of the R24, although it had a larger inlet valve, and the thing was supposed to do 95 km/h (59 mph) which is not bad for half a motorcycle. That, after all, is what it amounted to; and a new system of type numbering conceded the fact in 1951 when a few detail changes made it the R25/2.

Of course there had to be an R25/3, but really that was a much more developed machine with light-alloy wheel rims, central brakes in light-alloy hubs, new telescopic forks of greater travel (and at long blessed last some hydraulic damping to keep them under control), and much better overall proportions with the adoption of 18-inch wheels, an inch smaller in diameter than before. Technically the most interesting feature was a very long inlet tract, which elbowed its way up from the carburettor entry and climbed up the top tube of the frame .between the draperies of the fuel tank, to finish at an air filter behind the steering head. The length of this pipe, including the carburettor and the inlet port in the cylinder head, was 70 cm (27 in), so long that it smoothed out the pressure pulses at the filter and thus improved filter efficiency. It also enabled the oscillations of the air column in this long tract to be tuned for resonance, improving the power incidentally but the torque particularly.

This was a new science, even though British protagonists of the highly tuned unsupercharged engine had made a good empirical start with it in the 1930s. In those days it was accepted more or less as a matter of course in Germany and Italy that if you wanted a really powerful engine—for competition or high-altitude flight or any other circumstance when the simple admission of the atmosphere through a hole was inadequate—the proper forcing tool to use was a supercharger. Much of the work done by Schleicher on the competition BMW motorcycles had been to this end; and of course the aero-engines became more and more highly supercharged as time went on, culminating practically in the mighty 801 radial and pragmatically in the almost preposterous 803. This latter engine is scarcely known and came about in interesting circumstances, following the issue in 1943 of a directive to the German aero-engine industry to the effect that they had better get busy on evolving a class of engines which would begin at about 4000 horsepower and extend, with coupling if necessary, up to 10,000. Some weird and wonderful machines were postulated by Daimler-Benz and by DVL, the German equivalent of the Royal Aircraft Establishment, most of them grotesque but one or two really elegant. Then BMW came along and wiped all their eyes with the 803, which was simply two of their 14-cylinder radials joined on a common axis and producing 3950 horsepower without any increase in frontal area compared with the basic engine. Unlike most of the others, this was not so much a design study, it was an engine which was built and which worked—but as things turned out it did not matter a great deal, for instructions were issued for all work on the new class of engines to be suspended forthwith in the summer of 1944. BMW might well have been largely responsible for that suspension; their axial-flow gas turbine was coming along remarkably well.

A gas turbine was tantamount to a big efficient supercharger with an afterburner and turbine, and its high-altitude superiority over the piston engine and airscrew gave an ironic twist to the aviation career of BMW which, it will be remembered, began with unsupercharged piston engines specifically intended for high-altitude work. Now in these new post-war years BMW were back with unsupercharged engines again, whether they liked it or not, for forced induction was proscribed from racing and could hardly be contemplated for anything else.

Mastering the new science was the task of Alex von Falkenhausen, a nobleman from Schwabing. He had started with two-wheelers: in 1934 this Frankonian baron refused an offer by the celebrated

Professor Willy Messerschmitt and joined BMW as a designer in the motorcycle section. He brought with him considerable experience, including about a hundred assorted first prizes achieved mainly on two wheels but also on four, alone or with his wife Kitty as partner. In 1943 von Falkenhausen took over the entire BMW motorcycle test programme, and his hand is imprinted on all the post-war BMW 'bikes up to the end of the 1960s, just as it is on all BMW engines produced since—for in 1958 he became head of engine development.

Among the single-cylinder machines, both the motor and the cycle enjoyed quite intense development in the latter 1950s. The new range of Earles-forked swinging-arm twins that appeared in 1955 was complemented by the similarly sprung R26, now with 15 horsepower at 6400 rpm. These figures sounded high but were eclipsed in 1960 when the last of the half-bikes came into being, still a 68 x 68 mm 250 but now developing 18 bhp at 7400 rpm. It was in other words no longer half an R50, but more like half an R50S, though the latter had a higher compression ratio and developed its peak power at 7650 rpm. The real difference of course was that the twin did not vibrate. The single could not be felt to vibrate, which is rather a different matter: the entire engine and gearbox assembly was flexibly borne in rubber mountings.

This was a good idea if not a new one: though Norton were not to pursue it further in their Commando for years to come, Sunbeam had done it fourteen years earlier and the need for it had been explained as early as 1920 by Mr. Douglas Leechman in an I.Mech.E. paper: *The engine is no inert mass, but a powerful generator struggling at every explosion to rotate backwards round its crankshaft, and wrenching some thousands of times a minute at the fixtures which attempt to retain it in place. A body of such active nature is essentially unsuited to form one of the elements of a frame, the functions of which are characteristic to those of a passive resistor.*

In the case of a single-cylinder engine that is putting it mildly, for the thing vibrates in most available directions, taking its exhaust pipe and all other accoutrements with it. On the R27 they all had to be isolated: nothing could be allowed to pass from the engine to the frame except through a generously cushioning layer of rubber that had to be inspected for wear and degradation every 10,000 miles.

Whether despite or because of the flexibly mounted engine making no contribution to the stiffness of the frame, the R27 was, as lightweights go—and at 162 kg (356 lb) it was heavy for a 250—a particularly sturdy machine with all the air of solid imperturbability that had long been part of the BMW character. It had to be, for the instructions in the owner's manual almost encouraged him to fit a sidecar; and maybe this was why bottom gear was so dreadfully low. In the R26 it had been even worse; but at least such low gearing would have had virtues for the sportsman who, particularly in the USA, chose the BMW 250 for rough-riding events, most notably that American phenomenon, John Penton, who rode one in the International Six Days event when in 1965 the USA sent a team to the Isle of Man.

In general, however, sportsmen were not attracted to the small-capacity BMWs, which were essentially refined tourers for those whose appetite for speed was modest and whose desire for quality could not be met by anything else in the lightweight class. Such customers were becoming more and more difficult to find in the 1960s, when the motorcycle as a means of transport was growing less and less fashionable, when even the Bundeswehr was only interested in a limited run of lightweight cross-country specials. After a total production of only 15,364 in nearly eight years, the quietest, smoothest, and most sophisticated single-cylinder machine of its time was finished. The BMW design was too expensive in this class, and the decision was taken in 1967 that the R27 had been the last of the small singles. At the time, BMW were having to ask themselves whether they were justified in continuing the manufacture of any motorcycles at all.

	R39	R2	R4
ENGINE Type Number	M40	M67 S1	M69 S1
Cylinders, bore, stroke mm	1x68x68	1x63x64	1x78x84
Displacement cm^3	247	198	398
Compression ratio :1	6	6.7	5.7
Valve location	oh	oh	oh
Camshaft(s)	1	1	1
Carburettor	BMW	Sum	—
Power PS max	6.5	6	12
at rev/min	4000	3500	3500
Corresponding bmep kg/cm^2	6	7.9	7.86
Oil capacity, litres	2	1.5	1.75
TRANSMISSION Type Number	G41	G67 S1	G69
Gear Ratios :1 i	2.26	2.89	2.9 • 3.6
top gear ii	1.55	1.7	1.5 • 2.18
iii	1	1	1 • 1.35
iv			• 1
Final drive ratio :1	2.65	6.75	5.11 or 5.63
CHASSIS Type Number	R39	F67 S1	F69 S1
Frame	tubular double loop	Star pressed steel	Star pressed steel
Front forks	trailing bottom link	trailing bottom link	trailing bottom link
springing	leaf	leaf	leaf
damping	friction	friction	friction
Rear forks	unsprung	unsprung	unsprung
springing	—	—	—
damping	—	—	—
Front brake type	drum 1LS	drum 1LS	drum 1LS
diameter mm	151	200	200
Rear brake type	transmission band	drum 1LS	drum 1LS
Tyre	27x3.5 or 26x3	25x3 SS	26x3.50 SS
Fuel tank, litres	10	11	12
Weight, kg	110	110	137
Maximum speed km/h	100	95	100
Frame numbers	8000-8900	P15000-19260	—
Engine numbers	36000-36900	101-4260	—
Quantity built	900	—	15200
Years of production	1925–7	1931–6	1932–8

	R3	R35	R20
ENGINE Type Number	203/1	235/1	220/1
Cylinders, bore, stroke mm	1x68x84	1x72x84	1x60x68
Displacement cm^3	305	340	192
Compression ratio :1	6	6	6
Valve location	oh	oh	oh
Camshaft(s)	1	1	1
Carburettor	Sum	Sum	Amal or Bing
Power PS max	11	14	8
at rev/min	4200	4500	5400
Corresponding bmep kg/cm^2	7.84	8.35	7.04
Oil capacity, litres	1.75	1.75	1.5
TRANSMISSION Type Number	204/5	204/5	220/1
Gear ratios :1 i	3.6	3.6	2.77
ii	2.18	2.18	1.57
iii	1.35	1.35	1
iv	1	1	1
Final drive ratio :1	5.11 or 5.63	5.63	4.18
CHASSIS Type number	203/1	235/1	220/1
Frame	Star pressed steel	Star pressed steel	tubular double-loop, bolted
Front forks	trailing bottom link	telescopic	telescopic
springing	leaf	internal helical	internal helical
damping	friction	none	none
Rear forks	unsprung	unsprung	unsprung
springing	—	—	—
damping	—	—	—
Front brake type	drum 1LS	drum 1LS	drum 1LS
diameter mm	200	160	160
Rear brake type	drum 1LS	drum 1LS	drum 1LS
Tyres	3.5x26	3.50x19	3.00x19
Fuel tank, litres	12.5	12	12
Weight, kg	149	155	130
Maximum speed km/h	100	100	95
Frame numbers	P1001-1740	300001-315654	100001-105029
Engine numbers	20001-20740	300001-315387	100001-105004
Quantity built	740	15387	5000
Years of Production	1936	1937−40	1937−8

		R23	R24
ENGINE Type Number		223/1	224/1
Cylinders, bore, stroke mm		1x68x68	1x68x68
Displacement cm^3		247	247
Compression ratio :1		6	6.75
Valve location		oh	oh
Camshaft(s)		1	1
Carburettor		Amal or Bing	Bing
Power PS max		10	12
at rev/min		5400	5600
Corresponding bmep kg/cm^2		6.84	7.92
Oil capacity, litres		1.5	1.5
TRANSMISSION Type Number		220/1	224/1
Gear Ratios :1	i	2.77	3.96
top gear	ii	1.57	1.95
	iii	1	1.32
	iv	1	1
Final drive ratio :1		4.18	4.18
CHASSIS Type Number		220/1	224/1
Frame		tubular double-loop bolted	tubular double-loop bolted
Front forks		telescopic	telescopic
springing		internal helical	internal helical
damping		none	none
Rear forks		unsprung	unsprung
springing		—	—
damping		—	—
Front brake type		drum 1LS	drum 1LS
diameter mm		160	
Rear brake type		drum 1LS	drum 1LS
Tyres		3.00x19	3.00x19
Fuel tank, litres		9.6	12.
Weight, kg		135	130
Maximum speed km/h		90	95
Frame numbers		106001-114203	200001-212007
Engine numbers		106001-114021	200001-212007
Quantity built		8000	12007
Years of Production		1938–41	1949

	R25	R25/2	R25/3
ENGINE Type Number	224/2	224/2	252/1
Cylinders, bore, stroke mm	1x68x68	1x68x68	1x68x68
Displacement cm^3	247	247	247
Compression ratio :1	6.5	6.5	7.
Valve location	oh	oh	oh
Camshaft(s)	1	1	1
Carburettor	Bing	Bing	Bing or Sawe
Power PS max	12	12	13
at rev/min	5600	5800	5800
Corresponding bmep kg/cm^2	7.92	7.65	8.28
Oil capacity, litres	1.25	1.25	1.25
TRANSMISSION Type Number	224/2	224/2	224/2
Gear ratios :1 i	3.96	3.96	3.96
top gear ii	1.95	1.95	1.95
iii	1.32	1.32	1.32
iv	1	1	1
Final drive ratio :1	4.5 or 5.2	4.5 or 5.2	4.16 or 4.8
CHASSIS Type Number	224/2	224/2	225/3
Frame	tubular double-loop	tubular double-loop	tubular double-loop
Front forks	telescopic	telescopic	telescopic
springing	internal helical	internal helical	internal helical
damping	none	none	hydraulic
Rear forks	plunger	plunger	plunger
springing	internal helical	internal helical	internal helical
damping	none	none	hydraulic
Front brake type	drum 1LS	drum 1LS	drum 1LS
diameter mm			
Rear brake type	drum 1LS	drum 1LS	drum 1LS
Tyres	3.25x19	3.25x19	3.25x18
Fuel tank, litres	12	12	12
Weight, kg	140	142	150
Maximum speed km/h	95	95	119
Frame numbers	220001-243400	—	284001-331705
Engine numbers	220001-243400	—	284001-331705
Quantity built	23405	38651	47700
Years of Production	1950	1951—3	1953—5

	R26	R27
ENGINE Type Number	224/5	226/2
Cylinders, bore, stroke mm	1x68x68	1x68x68
Displacement cm^3	247	247
Compression ratio :1	7.5	8.2
Valve location	oh	oh
Camshaft(s)	1	1
Carburettor(s)	Bing	Bing
Power PS max	15	18
at rev/min	6400	7400
Corresponding bmep kg/cm^2	8.66	8.99
Oil capacity, litres	1.25	1.25
TRANSMISSION Type Number	224/3	226/2
Gear ratios :1 i	3.59	3.59
top gear ii	1.96	1.96
iii	1.32	1.32
iv	1	1
Final drive ratio :1	4.16 or 5.2	4.16 or 5.2
CHASSIS Type Number	224/3	226/2
Frame	tubular double-loop	tubular double-loop
Front forks	Earles	Earles
springing	helical	helical
damping	hydraulic double-acting	hydraulic double-acting
Rear forks	trailing fork	trailing fork
springing	helical	helical
damping	hydraulic	hydraulic
Front brake type	drum 1LS	drum 1LS
diameter mm		
Rear brake type	drum 1LS	drum 1LS
Tyres	3.25x18	3.25x18
Fuel tank, litres	15	15
Weight, kg	158	162
Maximum speed km/h	128	130
Frame numbers	340005-370242	372001-387364
Engine numbers	340005-370242	372001-387364
Quantity built	30238	15364
Years of Production	1955—60	1960—7

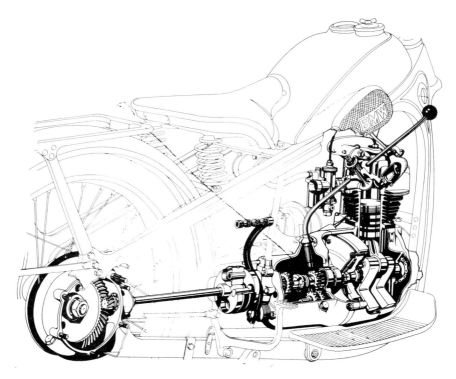

Straight-line drive in the R2.

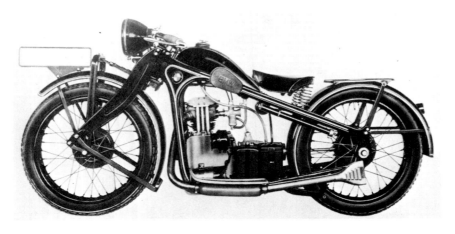

R2

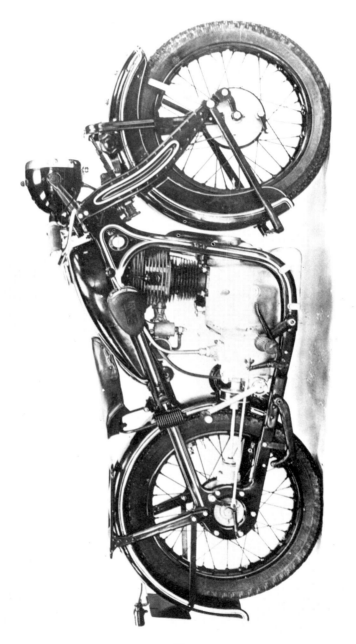

R4 of 1934

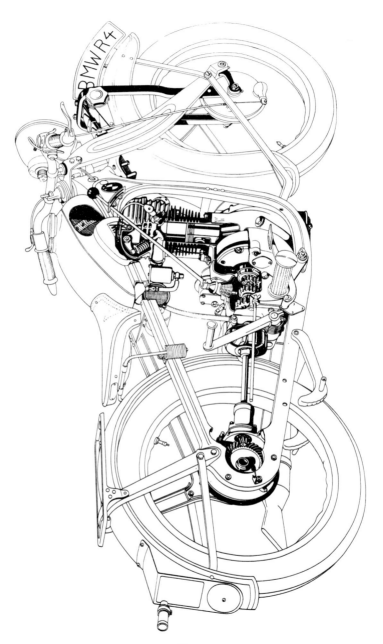

Engine and drive-line of the R4.

R3 of 1936

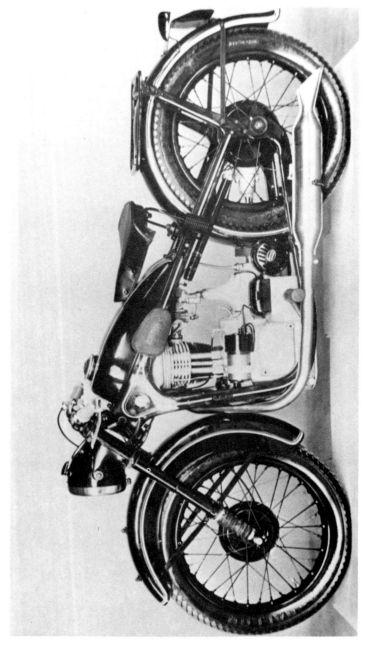

R35

R35 in utility finish, which highlights the aluminium-alloy head.

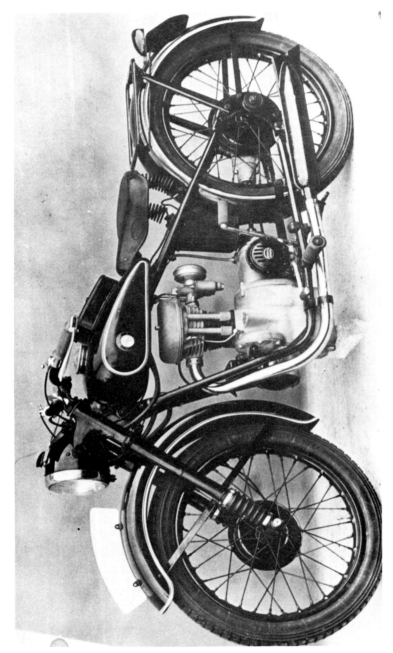

R.20

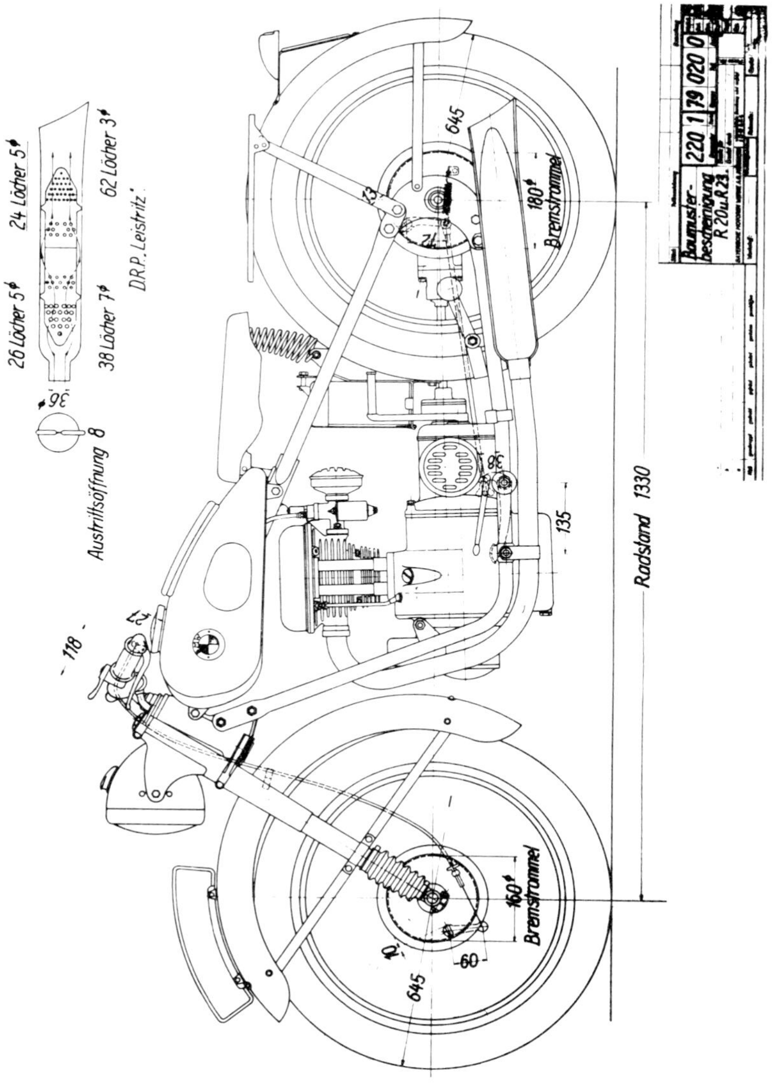

24 Löcher 5∮

26 Löcher 5∮

62 Löcher 3∮

38 Löcher 7∮

D.R.P. Leistritz

Austrittsöffnung 8

3,6

Bremstrommel

180∮

135

Radstand 1330

645

118

Bremstrommel

160∮

60

645

Baumuster-
beschreibung
R 20 u. R 23.

220 1 79 020 0

R 20/23

Dated 23 January 1939, this photograph is of an experimental version of the R36. The important feature is the cylinder head, modelled on that of the Pratt & Whitney Hornet aero-engine, which BMW had been building successfully under licence. The Hornet head was forged and had uncommonly effective cooling; in the motorcycle head, temperature gradients were controlled by setting the exhaust port to face the rear, where it discharged into an extensively shielded exhaust pipe and silencer.

R24

R25/2 in utility finish, with high-level exhaust and unflared front mudguard as further distinguishing features.

R26

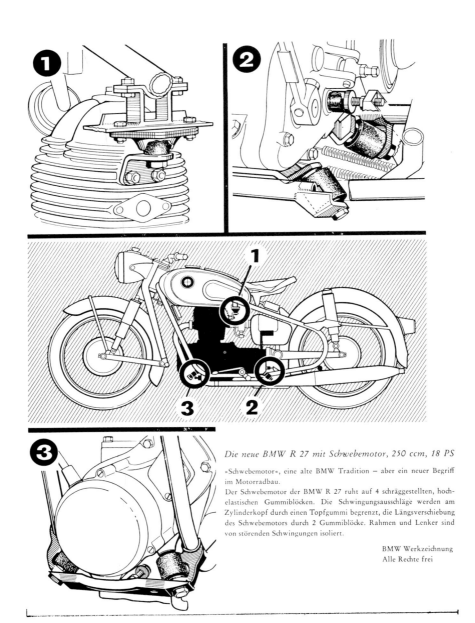

Die neue BMW R 27 mit Schwebemotor, 250 ccm, 18 PS

»Schwebemotor«, eine alte BMW Tradition – aber ein neuer Begriff im Motorradbau.
Der Schwebemotor der BMW R 27 ruht auf 4 schräggestellten, hochelastischen Gummiblöcken. Die Schwingungsausschläge werden am Zylinderkopf durch einen Topfgummi begrenzt, die Längsverschiebung des Schwebemotors durch 2 Gummiblöcke. Rahmen und Lenker sind von störenden Schwingungen isoliert.

BMW Werkzeichnung
Alle Rechte frei

Rubber mounting of the R27 engine required elaborate brackets. Note the longitudinal snubbers in details 2 and 3:

CHAPTER 4

WAR AND PIECES

During and after the Normandy landings by which the Allies began their invasion of occupied France in 1944, the battleship HMS Rodney stood off the French shore providing the sort of bombardment that only she and her sister-ship Nelson, with nine 16-inch guns apiece, were equipped to deliver. There was a stage in the proceedings when the bombardment had been eased, and after a time only one of the Rodney's guns was active, lobbing 1-ton shells inland with apparently monotonous regularity under the guidance of a small spotter aircraft which after every bang would radio back the instruction 'Up a thousand!' Then there would come another bang and again 'Up a thousand!' This went on for a while until it occurred to somebody in the Rodney to enquire what was going on—when it transpired that the line of craters stretching progressively further inland was tracing the course of a solitary and no doubt very frightened German despatch rider, who must have been wishing that he were astride a full-blown Rennsport BMW instead of the lowly standard Wehrmacht-issue machine he was riding!

In fact the most notable contribution by BMW to the motorcycling activities of the German forces during the war was not for solo riders but for the sidecar teams; and although, once it had got up steam in the highest of its eight forward gears, it could reach a rousing 95 km/h or thereabouts (60 mph), the R75 was not built for speed. It was not even built as a motorcycle to which a sidecar might be attached as an afterthought, as was the R71 which had to serve until the new machine was ready late in 1940. The R75 was a complete cross-country vehicle, with a driven sidecar wheel and a complex trans-mission embodying a two-stage range-change gearbox with four off-highway gears, four road gears, two reverse gears, and a lockable differential for the sidecar drive. This extensive range of options, from a crawler gear to an overdrive, was as necessary as the fat tyres on their 16-inch wheels to the ability of the rugged combination to keep going over the variously difficult terrains of the Russian plains, the Finnish tundra, the North African desert and the French Maritime Alps. The outfit weighed no less than 400 kg (880 lb) and needed all the 26 bhp of the overhead valve 750 cc engine. It was a lot of weight to stop, too, and the combination had hydraulic brakes as yet another item in the list of technical niceties, which included (for the first time on the flat twins) an automatic centrifugal advance mechanism built into the magneto which had been moved to the front of the crankshaft.

It was all very clever, but it was no more than a minor feature of a necessarily major commitment to the *parabellum* industry. Undoubtedly BMW's greatest contribution was in aero-engines, with the 801 radial and the 109-003 gas turbine; and it was work on these that occupied the largest staff (47,346 employees) in its history. While they laboured, it was the princely R66, the redoubtable supercharged Rennsport, and the nimble and gratifyingly sporting 2-litre cars (with a clever cylinder head designed by Schleicher) whose imperishable image lingered to preserve BMW's reputation as vehicle manufacturers as high as it possibly could be through all the years of war and subsequent restoration.

There was plenty of restoring to be done. In the closing stages of the war the factory was absolutely plastered by Allied bombers, and not a great deal was left. Whatever remained was officially doomed: on 11 April 1945 Hitler's order encoded as *Tilly* was delivered to the BMW board: all production facilities were to be destroyed immediately.

Kurt Donath, then chief of BMW, ignored the order. His fellow member of the board, Arthur Scholl, had a few months earlier boldly asked for 60 million Reichsmarks from Marshall Göring. He got it— possibly because Göring had a soft spot for BMW, dating from nearly twenty years earlier when he had been one of the outstanding leaders of the Richthofen wing, whose fighters were powered by BMW engines. Now, with another war about to be lost, Donath took the long-term view that the self-destruction ordered by the Führer would be more than necessarily suicidal. *On ne meurt qu'une fois,* as

Molière wrote, *et c'est pour si longtemps!* Donath and Scholl together managed to preserve everything possible, even when Hitler's order was repeated, with acquisitive overtones, by the Deputy Commander of the American garrison in Munich: on 1 October 1945, Eugene Keller Jnr commanded the dismantling and destruction of the factory, anything usable to be shipped to Detroit.

They managed to skate around that one, too; but inevitably a lot was lost. All the gear for building cars and motorcycles had been shifted to the old Dixi factory at Eisenach, which subsequently found itself east of the line drawn between the Russians and the rest. It was hardly surprising that the vehicles built there after the war were recognisably BMWs: in fact the cars were the pre-war designs, and the Russians are still making their Ural motorcycle, the engine of which is substantially that of the R66 and the frame of which is substantially that of the later R67/R52 series. All that was possible for BMW to make in Munich was pots and pans. It was the 1919 story all over again, production depending on what could be found amongst the scrap that could be profitably converted. Cooking pots, bakers' dough-making utensils, simple agricultural machinery—it was poor work for a factory that had once turned out beautiful turbine blades and roller-bearing crankshafts, but it was better than none.

Not until 1948 did the occupying powers concede that BMW might once again make motorcycles. As already related, the concession was strictly limited, with the intention that only utilitarian and economical lightweights should be produced. The little R24 was rather utilitarian, for all the customary sober dignity of its appearance: it was made with the most primitive tools and jigs in a very make-shift machine-shop. At least the selling of the machines was no problem: it was more a matter of making such allocations as were possible. Over 9000 were produced in 1949, and gradually production facilities were improved. Other things were improving significantly too, as the German Mark regained its status as a hard currency. With the outlook becoming more favourable, the company could be permitted to extend its operations to include their traditional two-cylinder motorcycles.

Understandably, the first corresponded substantially to a pre-war

model, the R51/2 built in 1950 being just what the numbers implied—
a variant of the 1938 model. There were some differences: for the
first time, inclined downdraught carburettors were specified. As the
drive chain for the two camshafts of the pre-war model did not meet
new requirements in respect of durability and quietness, the engine
was converted to a single camshaft with spur gear drive, as in the days
before 1936. It meant that the reciprocating weight of the valve gear
would be greater, but this handicap was reduced by carving surplus
weight out of the tappets. At whatever cost, it seemed that BMW
would cling to their ohv designs, and so it turned out: not since the
end of the war have BMW built a side-valved motorcycle. Even when
there was a demand for a heavy-duty sidecar machine, it was the
overhead-valve R67 with 600 cc engine that served. 'The angel of
the road', it was called, for it was the workhorse of the gangs of men
who were sent out to repair the ravaged highways. Nowadays, BMW
advertising tells us that *it takes one to catch one:* then, it took
one to make way for one.

R75

ENGINE Type Number	275/2
Cylinders, bore, stroke mm	2x78x78
Displacement cm^3	745
Compression ratio : 1	5.6 – 5.8
Valve location	oh
Camshaft(s)	2
Carburettor(s)	2 Graetzin
Power PS max	26
at rev/min	4000
Corresponding bmep kg/cm^2	7.96
Oil capacity, litres	2

TRANSMISSION Type Number		275/1
Gear ratios : 1	i	3.6
top gear	ii	2.05
	iii	1.35
	iv	1
Reverse		−2.66

all subject to 1.38:1 range change

Final drive ratio : 1	6.05 until No. 754057, then 5.69
Frame	tubular with sidecar chassis
Front forks	telescopic
springing	internal helical
damping	hydraulic
Rear forks	unsprung
Sidecar springing	none
Front brake type	drum 1LS
diameter mm	250
Rear brake type	drum 1LS
Tyres	4.50x16
Fuel tank, litres	24
Weight, kg	420
Maximum speed km/h	95
Frame Numbers	750001-
Engine Numbers	750001-
Quantity built	16500
Years of Production	1941

Shorn of its sidecar the R75 looks fearsome, complex and in some ways unorthodox. The power take-off for the sidecar wheel is just ahead of the rear hub centre.

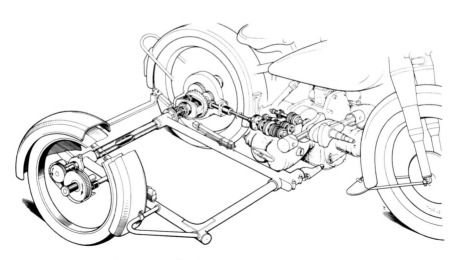

R75 drive lines and outrigger chassis.

CHAPTER 5

KEEPING THE FAITH

. . . and there is no new thing under the sun. Is there a thing whereof men say, 'See, this is new?' It has been already, in the ages which were before us. Ecclesiastes is always topical, as much today as at any other time in BMW history, particularly 1955 when the new range of Earles-forked motorcycles appeared. Ernest Earles was an Englishman whose intriguing front fork design, featuring long leading links from the bottom of backswept stanchions, had attracted more than a little attention, most significantly from the MV Agusta racing team and perhaps least so from Douglas, whose Dragonfly was one of the few motorcycles then sharing with BMW the distinction of a transverse flat-twin engine. (As an historical aside, it is worth noting that the others found their customers almost entirely among police forces—the Swiss for Condor, the French for Ratier—and in due course BMW were to find themselves in the same plight.)

The Earles forks that made the 1955 range of BMWs look so new were not so new. In a motorcycling magazine published in Britain in 1926, I found a drawing of a motorcycle suspension layout proposed by a reader—and the front forks were pure Earles. In that same year, the TT Scott was running with its own peculiar brand of telescopic forks embraced by a girder-like set of tubes and with a central spring. Nine years later, BMW pursued the latter idea further: twenty years later still, they latched on to the other.

The spirit of the times in Germany was such as to prompt the expectation of something new. In the early 1950s the country presented an almost incredible sight: all the work in the fields was being done by women, even the ploughing, because all the men were hard at it in the factories and on the building sites. The shop windows in the big cities were impressively filled and handsomely lit, and it was only if the shopper chanced to look up that he noticed the higher storeys were still no more than a gutted shell of what had once been a substantial block. The whole situation was summed up in a scene that still illuminates the recollection: a gleaming new Mercédès-Benz 300 saloon parked against the sombre backdrop of a battered but once glorious Köln cathedral. BMW for their part were renewing themselves by repeating themselves.

Motorcycle sales in the early 1950s suggested that they were doing the right thing: by 1953 Munich had sold its 100,000th motorcycle since the end of the war. The R51/2 and R67 may have been essentially pre-war designs, but development work showed up in details. Hydraulic bump stops were incorporated in the dampers of the front forks, the brakes were widened and the front brake made fiercer and more powerful by conversion to the principle of two leading shoes. Because the R67 was meant for sidecar haulage it kept its steel wheels, but the R51 acquired light-alloy rims with the added safety and strength imparted by straight-ended spokes. Those alloy rims were all that was necessary to complete the impression of high quality and high performance potential; and since nobody was in any doubt about the former, it remained only to confirm the latter by the introduction of the 35 bhp R68 which, with its 600 cc engine able to run up to 7000 rpm, was the first production BMW capable of 100 mph.

At this stage the market would have been ready for something entirely new. The fact that they did not get it may be blamed on the company's stifling conservatism, lack of salesmanship, or failure to undertake reasonable market research. Indeed they had suffered severe loss of confidence, because although their motorcycles had done so well up to 1953, sales of them had nose-dived since—and a slump in motorcycles was a slump indeed, for the revival of car production in the winter of 1951 had failed to produce the profit anticipated. It seemed that BMW were making the wrong cars in the wrong way at the wrong time, and although some of their new cars (notably the V8 type 507) earned great praise, they did not earn much money. To counteract this, the new motorcycles would have to be new enough but not too new: this was very satisfactorily achieved by making most of the changes apparent ones. In place of the obviously pre-war machines that had hitherto been available, the new 1955 models were based on a completely redesigned frame incorporating trailing-fork rear suspension and Earles-fork front suspension. The final drive shaft was no longer exposed but was enclosed in the right arm of the trailing forks, though curiously it remained separate in the similarly sprung Rennsport. All three new models had 18 inch wheels in place of the earlier 19 inch ones, twin leading shoes in the front brake, smaller mudguards, and larger silencers. The petrol tank was reshaped, and the traditional sprung saddle and separate pillion could be replaced by a stylish dualseat that was an optional extra. In this way the 500 cc R51/3 became the R50, the 600 cc R67/3 became the R60, and the R68 became the R69. Production of the R50 and the R60 was to drag on until 1969; but in 1960 the touring models received a power boost, at the same time as a sporting 500 (the R50S) was added to the range and the R69 likewise acquired an S suffix.

It was claimed that the reason for the new fully swinging frame was that further increases in suspension comfort, roadholding, and brake behaviour, were only possible with a basically new design. The swinging forks at each end of the chassis were sturdy affairs, pivoting in adjustable taper-roller bearings to ensure that their mounting was free from play and to facilitate response to the smallest road irregularity by eliminating the parasitic spring rate that might be introduced by less frictionless bearings. Given these premises it became possible to employ progressive-rate springs, and these were neatly concealed within the dust covers of the hydraulic dampers to constitute complete suspension strut units that were easily replaced or adjusted. To ensure the necessary comfort, the initial rate of the springs was so low that wheel travel became quite considerable, spring travel amounting to 129 mm. This could have led to severe and discommoding oscillations in pitch during acceleration or braking, but the effects of weight transfer in these circumstances were offset not only by a low centre of gravity of the sprung mass and by a long wheelbase but also by anti-dive front and anti-squat rear geometry: front brake torque was applied through the leading link and tended to raise the nose of the machine in opposition to the depression induced by forward weight transfer during deceleration, while the torque reaction from the final-drive bevels was similarly harnessed astern. The torque delivered to those bevels would be shock-free, for there was a completely new three-shaft gearbox with a powerful spring-loaded face-cam shock absorber on the primary shaft.

Other damping devices appeared with the R69S, the first production motorcycle to have an hydraulic steering damper. Its engine, which ran up to 7000 rpm to develop 42 bhp, bore a vibration damper on its crankshaft. It was also a sobering thought that the rear main bearing was redesigned (a floating barrel-roller bearing instead of ball races) to accommodate crankshaft flexure, as was done in the overhead-camshaft racing engines.

Even the best models looked and felt like tourers rather than like racers. This made it difficult to know by what standards to judge the range, especially in view of the higher prices asked for them. Should one compare them with other more mundane motorcycles, or should one reject the value-for-money criterion and judge them by absolute standards? There seemed something rather special about their engineering, something that implied a meticulous attention to detail and to finish, an innate compulsion to be absolutely thorough in the engineering of even the meanest component in a large and sophisticated complex. Where lesser manufacturers might make odds and ends out of sheet pressings, BMW offered costly forgings or elaborate castings. Where others would fob off cosmetically sensitive customers with a quick blow-over with metallic paint and some splashes of meretricious chromium, the BMW was dressed as expensively, as soberly and inconspicuously, as any Brummel could desire.

Alas, the brio seemed to have vanished with the barbarity. This made judgement even more difficult to arrive at, for although the performance of the sporting versions in particular was impressive, it could be matched by much cheaper machines made in England. They might not boast perfectly balanced flat-twin engines: indeed, they were likely to offer a vibro-massage from a thumping great single cylinder, or from an even larger vertical twin that was tantamount to two thumping singles in terms of vibration. They were dirty, messy, bitty and chain-driven; but they were also light, agile, wonderfully responsive and blessed with blissful gearchanges. By these contemporary and not entirely irrelevant standards, the BMWs were heavy and even dull.

To whom then did the all-swinging BMW of the all-swinging sixties appeal? There were few to be seen in Britain, simply because there were few people who, regardless of their inclinations to purchase this or that kind of motorcycle, had the means to buy one so costly. There were but few to be seen in Germany either, and most of those were in the hands of the highway police: in Germany's industrial west, at any rate, one did not then see people riding motorcycles ostensibly for pleasure, and the ton-up man was conspicuous by his absence.

Whoever he might be, the BMW rider was presumably a burly individual. Things are different today (except where BMWs are concerned) but then it seemed that 200 kg (440 lb) was an awful lot or iron to manhandle on to its centre stand—and there was no prop stand to be footed featly by the frail and feeble.

The heaviness extended to almost everything that it was the rider's concern to use. The clutch was not too bad, but neither the hand-brake, the throttle, nor the gear pedal, responded at all well to the gnarled fist in the velvet glove: only by discarding the velvet glove might you begin to get results. To the solid *Bayerische Bauer*—a long-armed short-necked species, traditionally supposed by non-Bavarians to be three-quarters-of-a-German high and a German-and-a-half wide—this was presumably no impediment; but if you were delicately nurtured, one of those light-fingered individuals accustomed to the responsiveness of an agile British or Italian thoroughbred, the change to a BMW might be as disturbing as transferring from a Bugatti to a 'bus or from Manzanilla to a Guinness.

One must not be too caustic about this motorcycle. As with 'buses and Guinness, there was a lot to be said for it. The excellence of workmanship, the choice of materials, the quality of finish, were all of extremely high standard. Indeed there were probably no motor-cycles being made in any sort of production line anywhere in the world that could rival the R50/60/69S in these respects. Likewise, the quietness was such as only the anti-motorcycling lobby in Britain might ever have dreamed of, an absence not only of exhaust rumpus but also of intake whirr and of mechanical clatter. Those big silencers clearly did their job, even if they deteriorated faster than anything else on the 'bike. The Bosch electrics too were of refreshingly high quality, but again betrayed by the dull imprecise action of the controls and particularly by that infuriatingly hygroscopic plunger-action ignition switch in the headlamp shell.

Heavy and imprecise controls were part of the trouble with these old BMWs. The twistgrip in particular was very unsatisfactory: instead of acting directly upon the cable, it worked through a gearbox so made as to create a most undesirable amount of backlash in the system, so that initial rotation of the grip had no effect. Further rotation was low-geared, and the need to take a second fistful could make fast riding on give-and-take roads unnecessarily dangerous. Yet precise throttle control was desirable because of the pernickety nature of the then notorious BMW gearbox. It was not unreasonable that its ratios should be rather wide, so flexible were those engines; but though the ratios might suit the engines, their wideness and the heavy flywheel made each gearchange a slow and tedious business, despite the fact that the three-shaft layout left the selector dogs running at considerably less than engine speed.

In principle then, if not in detail, the swingers were clearly cast in a compulsively traditional mould; and this is something that demands examination, not only because of the marked differences between the BMW and conventional motorcycles, but also because sales had suffered such a sharp decline—and if it be argued that the decline was explicable in terms of social changes, it might be retorted that these should have been met by complementary changes in motorcycle design. Instead, the 1955-1969 BMWs represented nothing more than developments of a basic design that was well over thirty years old when they were new. Whether or not this might be a good thing is a topic for eternal debate; but at least if the basic concept remained unchanged after all that time, the details had been progressively and subtly changed, making it clear that the Bavarian engineer did not share the late Duke of Cambridge's antipathy to reform. It may be remembered that His Grace maintained that *All change, for whatever reason, is utterly to be deprecated.* However, one does not need to withdraw far from this intransigent position to qualify for a place among those who believe in *evolution,* the development of an existing concept to a high degree of refinement, rather than *revolution* which means starting with a clean sheet of drawing paper. Perhaps indeed the Germans felt with Pierre Vergnaud that *There was reason to fear that, like Saturn, the Revolution might devour each of its children in turn.* With so many more customers needed and so few to be found, BMW were possibly justified in not indulging in a technical breakaway, though their original design was sufficiently heterodox to remain so even in the 1960s, and even today.

One of its charms, provided the cylinders be not suffered to grow too large or lusty, is the horizontally opposed engine. This layout, known to continentals as the boxer, brings with it almost as a matter of course a perfection of balance that cannot be attained either in singles or in conventional vertical twins; even when the vertical twin is given crankpins at 180 degrees instead of 360, it is still usually left with a rocking couple of greater magnitude than that suffered by the flat twin, which has the advantage of having its cylinders more nearly in alignment—and the further advantage of resolving secondary vibrations in a way that the V twin cannot emulate. Another advantage of this engine layout is that it brings the heaviest parts of the structure low and so helps to keep the centre of gravity of the whole machine reasonably near the deck, and to reduce the pitching moment of inertia of the sprung mass. It also facilitates the use of shaft drive, the practical advantages of which are so great as unquestionably to justify the extra weight which it inevitably entrains. As for the torque reactions and gyroscopic precessions so often accused of exercising a destabilising influence, they would still be present if the crankshaft were disposed in any other conceivable plane, including the more conventional transverse one: the only difference is that felt by the rider unaccustomed to the characteristics of any particular layout, this being a counteraxiomatic case of unfamiliarity breeding contempt.

The regular BMW rider would find nothing amiss, whether he were tourer or sportsman. The R50 was of course the touring 500, the R60 its twenty per cent larger sister, and complementary to these two

were the R50S and R69S described as sports models by the manufacturers but still quite soft and tractable by the standards of the
really sporting rider. All four were essentially the same in construction:
the two sports models differed externally from the tourers in having
an hydraulic steering damper, a larger air-intake filter without a sliding
strangler, finned light-alloy nuts on the exhaust pipes, and cylinder
heads with fewer but sturdier fins. Of the two sports models the 600
differed externally from the 500 especially in the larger-diameter
intake pipes and the more convex rocker boxes. Of the tourers the
R50 could be recognised by the circular fins on each cylinder, whereas
its 600 cc counterpart had elliptical fins. Internally, differences in
valve gear, compression ratio, and one or two mechanical details
like the roller bearing at the rear of the crankshaft, enabled the
sports models to turn at speeds up to 7000 or 7650 rpm as against
the 5800 of the tourers. These differences might be translated into
something like a thirty per cent difference in power output; but if,
for example, the R50 was almost apologetically mild-mannered in
its generation of a mere 26 bhp, there were times when its gentleness
could be appreciated. As soon as the engine was started it would
settle down into the most fantastically slow and regular tickover.
One might quite easily count the individual firing impulses: this engine
made an industrial diesel sound like a Honda four by comparison.

   There was another structural feature in the engine that called for
comment, in the shape of the connecting rods. These drop forgings
were oval in cross section, much as one would expect in a two-stroke
engine but quite out of the ordinary in a four-stroke. The conventional
I-beam section is in fact incorrectly disposed to give the rod the
optimum beam stiffness for its duties, as a few specialist manufacturers
are beginning to appreciate now, but as was made clear many years
ago by Roland Cross in England and Charles Lafayette Taylor in
the USA. The elliptical-section BMW rod had the virtue of being
more streamlined as it cut through the air within the crankcase, and
thus reduced the pumping losses which are one of the gravest
handicaps of the horizontally opposed twin. A manufacturer of lesser
boxers, Douglas, learned the hard way at the beginning of the 1950s
that these pumping losses, aggravated by the fact that both pistons

moved inwards together to compress the air within the crankcase, could easily consume three bhp; but BMW forestalled this loss with the aid of a very large clack valve that popped open automatically whenever it was necessary to relieve internal pressure.

The same reduced windage losses explained the similar rods that flailed about inside the overhead-camshaft Rennsport or RS engines. Only thirty-two of these were originally built, the last of them in 1953, but plenty of spares and modifications were turned out consequently, notably when various forms of direct and indirect fuel injection were tried in the middle 1950s. The RS of 1953 was not a particularly impressive racer, developing only about 50 bhp; so, even before his retirement in the Senior T T of that year, the young German rider Walter Zeller did not attract any particular attention. It must be remembered, though, that motorcycle racing in Germany was then and is still very different from the frenzied and highly specialised sport that it has become in Britain and the USA. A rider there must be able to turn his hand to more kinds of competition than short-circuit racing, and the RS was designed for these other kinds as well—real road racing and daunting hillclimbs of the long-drawn-out Alpine variety. For these, a forgivingly torque-rich engine in a bicycle with a low centre of gravity and light weight is more effective than the conventionally peppery knife-edge circuit racer.

Consider for example the hillclimb at Freiburg, up 11½ km of German mountain. The sinuous road climbs up through the Black Forest, with a hundred and seventy-two curves and a gain in altitude of about 700 metres. The road is often narrow and its difficulties are emphasised by the low average speed of even the best competitors. When German champion Karl Hoppe set a new motorcycle record for the hill in 1966, he broke a record that was set no less than fifteen years earlier when Walter Zeller rode a BMW up at a speed a shade under 58 mph.

By 1956, Zeller's RS was a lot more powerful and he returned to the Isle of Man to put up a rousing performance in the Senior TT. A last-minute decision to run the machine without its fairing left it overgeared, despite which Zeller finished fourth at 94.69 mph behind the MV of John Surtees and the works Nortons of John Hartle and Jack Brett, with a fastest lap of practically 97 mph. It was no flash-in-the-pan result; despite the exceptional riders and redoubtable performance of the Italian fours, Zeller finished second in the Dutch TT and in the Belgian Grand Prix, came fifth in the Italian Grand Prix, and ended the season as runner-up to Surtees in the 500 cc World Championship. Two years later, a privately-owned RS carried Dickie Dale to third place in the 500 cc World Championship behind the MV team of Surtees and Hartle.

Surtees himself had been a BMW rider in continental events for a brief period between leaving the Norton team and joining MV Agusta, and so did two or three other displaced persons, including Geoffrey Duke and Fergus Anderson, the latter sadly killed while riding a BMW when he hit a kerbstone at Floreffe in Belgium. Broadly, however, there appears to be a trace of justification for the saying that you have to be either brave, mad, or German, to ride a solo BMW at race-winning speeds. Certainly the RS has been much more successful in racing sidecar outfits, where all of its characteristics rate as virtues and the cost of one of the specially modified engines with a centre main bearing (about 30,000 Dm even in 1971) was its greatest vice. Only twice since 1955 have BMW failed to win the sidecar TT for example, and the annals of the Grands Prix in that era make it clear that the BMW superiority in the World Championship was so great as to be downright boring. It is an unfair thing to say, perhaps, about a form of racing so exciting that a rider has to be brave and mad and German to do well. Indeed it has even been suggested that qualification may be yet more rigorous: it has been alleged that all the really quick drivers come from Hessen, a county in Bavaria . . .

With so few of the RS engines available, demand outstrips supply. Those who cannot find one or cannot afford one fall back on what are known in the jargon as 'roller' engines—highly-tuned short-stroke versions of the production pushrod engine, with roller-bearing cam followers allowing the exploitation of rather more extravagant cam profiles to the betterment of power and high-speed reliability alike. There are still several of these engines in circulation, apparently as enduring as those hoary old RS engines; but they cannot always be identified, having been built into standard production engine castings.

This may explain the occasionally surprising performance of ostensibly 'production' BMWs in the competition heyday of the R69S. It is known for example that the factory supplied a specially prepared engine for the assault by the English MLG Limited team on the 12 and 24-hour records in 1961. This machine had a Peel dolphin fairing, extra lamps, extra-high final drive gearing, and a riding position tailored for the racing crouch; but to a surprisingly large extent it was perfectly standard. Ridden by an English team comprising Sid Mizen, George Catlin, John Holder and Ellis Boyce, it contrived to average over 109 mph, including all pit stops, around the banked track at Montlhery, succeeding in taking the records in the 750 and 1000 cc classes. Shortly afterwards it was submitted to the weekly magazine MOTOR CYCLING for a road test, in the course of which it demonstrated a maximum speed just over 118 mph, together with a combination of stability, ride comfort, and braking power, that made a great impression on the testers. It emerged from this that, unlike the standard R69S engine, that of the record-breaker could be run continuously at 7000 rpm and briefly up to 7400; and although it was revealed that the megaphone exhausts employed at Montlhery yielded only 2 bhp more than the standard BMW silencers, the actual power output of the engine was evidently a factory-guarded secret. Could it have been a roller engine?

If it was, did it or a similar one power the MLG R69S that won the 500-miles Thruxton race in 1961, or the machine on which Peter Darvill and Norman Price won the 24-hours race at Barcelona in the same year? There need be no particular shame in the admission, for even if it turned out to be true it would still leave those BMWs considerably nearer to standard than most of the supposedly 'production' motorcycles with which they competed in these events. Certainly BMW's support for such racers was good in those times: that outstanding English rider David Degens, who rode an R69S in the 1963 Barcelona event early in a racing career which later led him to repeated wins on machines of his own construction, commented subsequently that the 'bike had not been free of trouble but that the service and support rendered by the factory was outstanding. The fact that he finished well placed, despite repeated stops for repairs and replacements (burnt-out dynamos were a recurrent problem, for instance), was ascribed by him much more to the BMW men at the pits than to the handling of the motorcycle itself.

The Barcelona circuit in twisty Montjuich Park is a particularly demanding one. Despite the impressive performances of BMWs there and in similar events such as the Bol d'Or, on more than one occasion in the R69S era, and despite the consistently meritorious performances of racing riders such as Zeller and Dale, the Earles-forked BMWs have come in for a lot of criticism of their handling.

The behaviour of an outright racer is always dependent on how it is set up and who is riding it. For the production machine there is less latitude, and in the over-the-counter swinging-fork BMWs there was room for criticism. The handling was fine on long fast steady-state bends, just as it was delightful when picking your way at little more than walking speed; but it was not a machine for twitching along a winding byroad. The ride was soft, well damped, so comfortable as to impart no clue as to the nature of the road surface, while the steering conspired with the suspension to keep the rider ignorant of this vital factor.

It was all part of a kind of remoteness, a desensitisation that extended throughout, even to those beautifully made controls—the forged levers, the geared twistgrip, even the petrol tap—which had none of the feel that one expects in well-bred machinery. It was as though one were to civilise a rifle by dulling its hair trigger.

It is not everybody who can be trusted with a hair trigger, and the BMW was above all things civilised. This was no nimble little dicer for twitching through the chicanery, but a hefty tourer that could nevertheless be heeled steeply over and kept there through a fast curve, either holding or modifying the chosen line as circumstances demanded. When (and only when) they were properly bedded in and adjusted, its brakes would atone for most of its other dynamic short-comings, and its steering was generally blameless at all speeds down to a standstill. Its proper métier was as a quietly competent master of the public highway, a Beautifully Made Wonderbike that would still be whispering through the traffic or charging the horizon when most of its rivals were languishing in the breakers' yards.

This was why the BMW became during this period the favourite mount, perhaps the only possible mount, of the really long distance rider. There were British servicemen who saw it as a pleasant way of coming home on leave from the Far East and returning, perhaps two or three times in a tour of duty. There were newspaper and press agency messengers who piled up enormous annual mileages in all weathers and swore by the machine's reliability, its reassuring ability to stay on the road—in all senses! Most dramatic of all, there were the long-distance loners of America.

The company had some enthusiastic dealers in the New World. One of them, Ed LaBelle of Philadelphia, took his RS production racer to Canada to win the national championship in 1958 and 1960. The intervening year saw his BMW finish 15th in the Formula 1 TT in the Isle of Man; and he was 20th in the more open Senior TT, an event so plagued by gale-force winds and icy rain that not many riders finished at all. That same year saw the appearance on the scene of John Penton, who spent 52 hours 11 minutes in riding an R69 from New York City to Los Angeles. His time was checked by Western Union, and constituted a new record for the transcontinental run, beating one of 76 hours established twenty years earlier; and bearing in mind that his time represented an average speed of 58.47 mph for the 3051 miles journey from coast to coast, it would be legally if not practically impossible to beat it today. At the time, Penton was a 33-year-old physical culture instructor with remarkable endurance: he took only 3 hours respite for sleep during the journey. When asked why he undertook it, he said that it was just for kicks— but before long he became a BMW dealer in Ohio, and an enthusiastic rider of the R27 in endurance events, winning the 500 miles Jack Pine Enduro and later representing his country in the ISDT. Meantime, other Americans were proving the endurance of the BMW over even longer distances: Daniel Liske of Nebraska set out from northern Alaska on an R60 and, six months and 95,000 miles later, arrived at the tip of South America. As a sequel he encompassed the 40,000 miles top-to-bottom transit of the Old World by riding from the northernmost point in Scandinavia to the southernmost of Africa.

If it were treated as it was meant to be treated, the BMW just seemed to go on and on, never breaking things, never sweating oil, never issuing more than the most apologetic murmur of exhaust noise. It was perhaps the most civilised motorcycle in the world. Yet although it inspired just faith it made few converts, and during the 1950s BMW began to find times hard, as an increasingly prosperous Germany acquired a taste for something bigger and better in *Prunkwagen* and spurned the motorcycle that had served it so well. Despite the introduction in 1955 of this range of quiet, impeccably mannered and beautifully finished luxury motorcycles of utterly distinctive specification and appearance, the end of the decade saw BMW's motorcycle sales topple; and the trend continued until, by the end of the 1960s, production was down to only 4700 a year. The cars, such as they were (and some of them were quite curious) were doing no better, and in 1959 it seemed that the end of the company was in sight. The last reserves were exhausted, the annual report closed in the red; and with the Bavarian government despairing of them and the financiers past caring, there was a strong possibility that BMW would sell their factory to Daimler-Benz who wanted it for lorry-building. Yet because the factory had kept up . their standards—above all in their motorcycles—refusing in any way to compromise whatever excellence they had attained, there were shareholders who kept up their support for everything that BMW represented. When those shareholders went into conference to fight for the existence of the company, they started by demanding postponement of the decision that appeared to be final, the decision to put an end to BMW. Even the Solex carburettor company took an interest, and when Dr Herbert Quandt declared himself ready to champion the BMW cause, the big banks regained their confidence in the firm's future.

In the design offices and the development department, work had already begun on the car that was to herald the *Neue Klasse,* the new range of saloons that would mark a new epoch for BMW, one in which it could be taken really seriously as a car manufacturer with a comprehensive model range. Despite the fact that these seeds had already been sown, it was inevitable in the circumstances that the managing director would have to go: and Hermann Richter-Brohm, who had enjoyed little success, bowed out. The new major share-holder, Dr Quandt, replaced him with Karl-Heinz Sonne.

The first car of the new range, the 4-door 1500 saloon, was announced in 1961 and was ballyhooed round the world. This car, with a clever engine and high implicit performance, with Michelotti styling and everybody's goodwill, was the first of the spritely, smart, aggressive and efficient series that proliferated to save the company and put them on the road to fame and fortune again, reversing the old philosophical procedure by turning accident into substance when BMW put their production up at the same time as all their rivals put their prices up.

When Sonne came on the scene in 1962, he introduced modern management methods which until that date had been quite foreign to the company's strategists. Cost accounting was a case in point, with which it could be established how much money each individual model variation cost and whether it produced any profit. Cost analysis established whether in production a cheaper material meeting the same quality standards would suffice. The traditionalists of the firm, who had nearly gone to the wall in defending their engineering against all comers, must have felt bitterly about what looked like becoming the age of the whizz-kid; but saviours have been crucified before.

The most important man in the new team under Sonne was Paul G. Hahnemann. Described as a man with a nose for niches, this new sales executive led BMW into a market gap with new sporty middle-class cars that were a tremendous success in 1963. But fancy BMW having a sales executive—the sales promotion techniques that Hahnemann introduced were as strange as all the other management techniques: the old tradition, that customers bought BMW but were not sold BMWs, had to go.

With it went the doubts and uncertainties, the crises and the creditors. By 1965 the company turnover was 593 million Marks, the output 58,524 vehicles, and the labour force had grown to 12,000. With a turnover per capita that had doubled in six years, the share-holders were getting a dividend, the 1963 distribution being the first in twenty years; and BMW were ploughing back millions into the company. They were concentrating on the cars that had made them solvent; but the motorcycles were suffering, almost being ignored. Production was steadily dropping, most of it going to police forces at home and abroad where the quietness, reliability and smart sobriety of the machines made them the ideal mounts of men whose job it was to impose or maintain at least some of the disciplines of civilisation. The days of the BMW motorcycle seemed to be numbered, however, and the management, intoxicated by cars, debated doing away with the two-wheelers. Their remaining customers were few, but were discerning and tasteful—and perhaps, since they were men of appreciable means if they could afford one of these impressively expensive machines, they were influential. It was a curious situation but in the long term a rewarding one, for whilst those riders remained faithful to BMW, the factory in turn was to remain faithful to them: instead of doing what had been threatened and closing down their motorcycle plant, BMW were to celebrate the revival of interest in motorcycling late in the 1960s with the perfectly timed production of brand new models produced in a new motorcycle factory, and to have that faith in turn rewarded by a monumental increase in sales.

	R51/2	R51/3	R67
ENGINE Type Number	254/1	252/1	267/1
Cylinders, bore, stroke mm	2x68x68	2x68x68	2x72x73
Displacement cm^3	494	494	590
Compression ratio :1	6.3	6.3	5.6
Valve location	oh	oh	oh
Camshaft(s)	2	1	1
Carburettor(s)	2 Bing	2 Bing	2 Bing
Power PS max	24	24	26
at rev/min	5800	5800	5500
Corresponding bmep kg/cm^2	7.65	7.65	7.31
Oil capacity, litres	2	2	2
TRANSMISSION Type Number	250/3	250/4	250/4
Gear ratios :1 i	2.77	2.77	2.77
top gear ii	1.75	1.75	1.75
iii	1.31	1.31	1.31
iv	1	1	1
Final drive ratio :1	3.89 or 4.62	3.89 or 4.57	3.56 or 4.38
CHASSIS Type Number	251/2	251/3	251/3
Frame	tubular cradle	tubular cradle	tubular cradle
Front forks	telescopic	telescopic	telescopic
springing	internal helical	internal helical	internal helical
damping	hydraulic	hydraulic double-acting	
Rear forks	plunger	plunger	plunger
springing	internal helical	internal helical	internal helical
damping	none	none	none
Front brake type	drum 1LS	drum 2LS	drum 2LS
diameter mm	200	200	200
Rear brake type	drum 1LS	drum 1LS	drum 1LS
Tyres	3.50x19	3.50x19	3.50x19
Fuel tank, litres	14	17	17
Weight, kg	185	190	192
Maximum speed km/h	140	140	140
Frame & Engine numbers	516001-521005	522001-526209	—
Quantity built	5050	18425	1470
Years of Production	1950	1951—4	1951

	R50	R69	R60
ENGINE Type Number	252/2	268/2	267/4
Cylinders, bore, stroke mm	2x68x68	2x73x73	2x73x73
Displacement cm^3	494	590	590
Compression ratio :1	6.8	8	6.5
Valve location	oh	oh	oh
Camshaft(s)	1	1	1
Carburettor(s)	2 Bing	2 Bing	2 Bing
Power PS max	26	35	28
at rev/min	5800	6800	5600
Corresponding bmep kg/cm^2	8.28	7.96	7.74
Oil capacity, litres	2	2	2
TRANSMISSION Type Number	245/1	245/1	245/1
Gear ratios :1 i	3.46	3.46.	3.46
top gear ii	1.96	1.96	1.96
iii	1.32	1.32	1.32
iv	1	1	1
Final drive ratio :1	3.18 or 4.25	3.18 or 4.25	2.91 or 3.86
CHASSIS Type Number	245/1	245/1	245/1
Frame	tubular looped	tubular looped	tubular looped
Front forks	Earles	Earles	Earles
springing	helical	helical	helical
damping	hydraulic, double-acting	hydraulic, double-acting	hydraulic, double-acting
Rear forks	trailing fork	trailing fork	trailing fork
springing	helical	helical	helical
damping	hydraulic	hydraulic	hydraulic
Front brake type	drum 2LS	drum 2LS	drum 2LS
diameter mm	200	200	200
Rear brake type	drum 1LS	drum 1LS	drum 1LS
Tyres	3.50x18*	3.50x18*	3.50x18*
Fuel tank, litres	17	17	17
Weight, kg	195	202	195
Maximum speed km/h	140	165	145
Frame numbers	550001-563515	652001-654955	618001-621530*
Engine numbers	550001-563515	652001-654955	622001-630000
Quantity built	32532	2819	20828
Years of Production	1955—69	1955—60	1956—67

*4.00x18 with sidecar

*up to 1960

	R67/2	R67/3	R68
ENGINE Type Number	267/2	267/2	268/1
Cylinders, bore, stroke mm	2x72x73	2x72x73	2x72x73
Displacement cm^3	590	590	590
Compression ratio :1	6.5	6.5	7.5—7.7
Valve location	oh	oh	oh
Camshaft(s)	1	1	1
Carburettor(s)	2 Bing	2 Bing	2 Bing
Power PS max	28	28	35
at rev/min	5600	5600	7000
Corresponding bmep kg/cm^2	7.74	7.74	7.74
Oil capacity, litres	2	2	2
TRANSMISSION Type Number	250/4	250/4	250/5
Gear ratios :1 i	2.77	2.77	3.08
ii	1.75	1.75	1.75
iii	1.31	1.31	1.31
iv	1	1	1
Final drive ratio :1	3.56 or 4.38	? 4.38	3.89
CHASSIS Type Number	251/3	251/3	251/4
Frame	tubular cradle	tubular cradle	tubular cradle
Front forks	telescopic	telescopic	telescopic
springing	internal helical	internal helical	internal helical
damping	hydraulic, double-acting	hydraulic, double-acting	hydraulic, double-acting
Rear forks	plunger	plunger	plunger
springing	internal helical	internal helical	internal helical
damping	none	none	none
Front brake type	drum 2LS	drum 2LS	drum 2LS
diameter mm	200	200	200
Rear brake type	drum 1LS	drum 1LS	drum 1LS
Tyres	3.50x19	F3.50x19 R4.00x18	3.50x19
Fuel tank, litres	17	17	17
Weight, kg	192	320 with sidecar	193
Maximum speed km/h	140	130 with sidecar	160
Frame & Engine numbers	—	—	650001-651453
Quantity built	4260	780	1453
Years of Production	1952—4	1955—6	1952—4

	R50S	R69S
ENGINE Type Number	252/3	268/3
Cylinders, bore, stroke mm	2x68x68	2x72x73
Displacement cm^3	494	590
Compression ratio :1	9.2	9.5
Valve location	oh	oh
Camshaft(s)	1	1
Carburettor(s)	2 Bing	2 Bing
Power PS max	35	42
at rev/min	7650	7000
Corresponding bmep kg/cm^2	8.45	9.28
Oil capacity, litres	2	2
TRANSMISSION Type Number	245/1	245/1
Gear ratios :1 i	3.46	3.46
top gear ii	1.96	1.96
iii	1.32	1.32
iv	1	1
Final drive ratio :1	3.58 or 4.33	3.13 or 4.33
CHASSIS Type number	245/2	245/2*
Frame	tubular looped	tubular looped
Front forks	Earles	†Earles
springing	helical	helical
damping	hydraulic, double acting	hydraulic, double acting
Rear forks	trailing fork	trailing fork
springing	helical	helical
damping	hydraulic	hydraulic
Front brake type	drum 2LS	drum 2LS
diameter mm	200	200
Rear brake type	drum 1LS	drum 1LS
Tyres	3.50x18S	3.50x18S
Fuel tank, litres	17	17
Weight, kg	198	202
Maximum speed km/h	160	175
Frame Numbers	564005-565639	655004-666320
Engine Numbers	622001-63000	622001-63000
Quantity built	1634	11417
Years of Production	1960—62	1960—69

*Late US models had 246 gearbox

†Late US models had telescopic front forks

R 51/2

R51/3

The BMW racers that became supreme in post-war sidecar racing were extensively derived from the pre-war overhead-camshaft machines. This one is crewed by Ludwig ('Wiggerl') Kraus and Bernhard Huser, winners of the 1951 German Grand Prix for 500cc combinations.

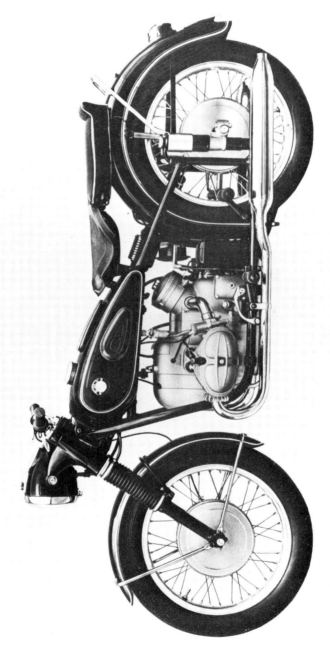

R68

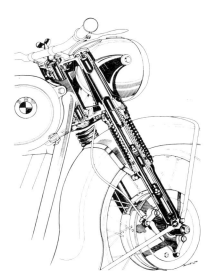

From 1951 to 1955 these telescopic front forks, featuring double-acting hydraulic damping and a simple friction steering damper, graced all the BMW twins. Note the twin leading-shoe operation of the brake, set in a hub providing for straight spokes.

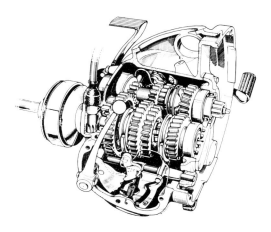

Twin-shaft gearbox of the R51/67/68

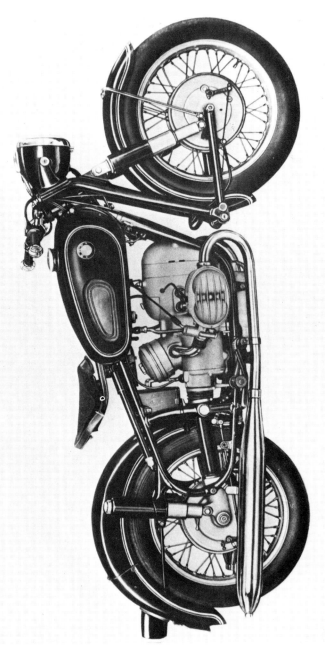

R 50/60

R69S

The Earles forks of 1955-69 were connected to an hydraulic steering damper on the R69S.

These forks belong to the R27 and might rightfully appear in ch.3, but they offer an instructive comparison here with those of the R69S in the preceding illustration. The friction damper for the steering is one of the few differences.

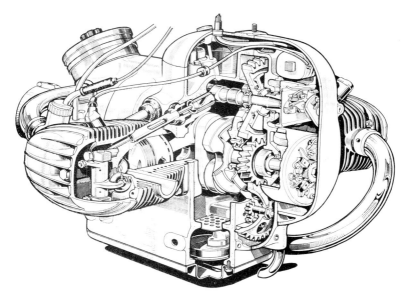

Features of the R50/60 engines included crankcase breathers high abaft and low before, solid-shanked connecting rods, and heavily ringed pistons.

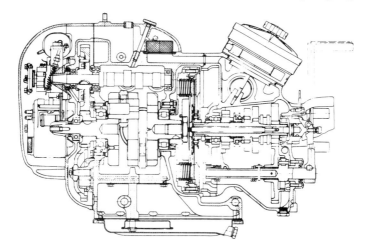

This drawing shows more conventional conrods, and also reveals the spherical-roller bearing at the rear of the crankshaft to accommodate flexure.

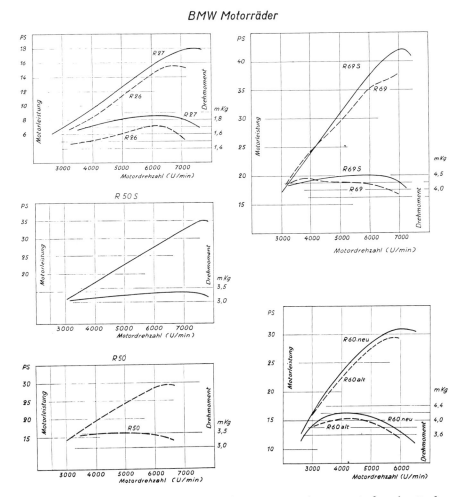

Curves for power (Motorleistung) and torque (Drehmoment) for the Earles-forked series reveal many different characters, the most impressive being the flat torque curve and consequently straight power curve for the high-revving R50S.

For real power and revs, there was always (and seemingly forever) the overhead-cam RS engine.

The RS was tried with fuel injection into the inlet ports or straight into the combustion chamber. It left the induction tracts beautifully uncluttered, and solved all problems of fuel surge such as bedevil sidecar racers.

The RS was more successful (on solo machines) with carburettors, and was one of the fastest bikes in the all-swinging 1950s.

The frames of some of the late Earles-forked RS models differed extensively from the production chassis, particularly at the extremities.

CHAPTER 6

THE SUPERBIKE REVIVAL

Hans-Gunther von der Marwitz, born into a distinguished family in 1927, was already a keen motorcyclist when he joined BMW in 1964 after working on engine development for Porsche. Whatever the conviction or resignation with which he accepts the Friz tradition today, he was not then at all enthusiastic about the kind of motorcycles represented by the Earles BMWs which were current at that time. When he tried one he thought it quite ghastly—and for however long the argument might continue to rage about the handling of the 1955-1969 BMWs, nobody could deny that he had been accustomed to something better. Motorcycling for him had meant racing around on his AJS 7R, with an occasional romp on a friend's G50 Matchless—crisp English classics, born to the scratching of Britain's short circuits and bred from a long line of Manx T T winners. Given the task of developing a new series of machines when BMW decided to stay in the motorcycle business, von der Marwitz had no doubts about what he wanted to achieve: *I wanted our new roadster to handle like the Manx Norton racer,* he told me: *I think we very nearly succeeded.*

Commercial success depended on the new machine being fairly lively, for liveliness was a characteristic rapidly returning to the market. As the 1960s progressed, the tremendous motorcycling boom in the USA promised to find an echo in Europe, and it looked as though there might be a bright future for top-notch big machines as well as for the spritely little traffic-cheaters with which the Japanese factories so profitably introduced America to the pleasures of two-wheeled travel. By 1965, when the BMW management were still wondering whether remaining in the motorcycle business would prove to be an inspired decision or a rash gamble, there were signs of an impending effloration of a whole new class of luxury high-performance motorcycles, as a dozen or so of manufacturers all around the world turned their speculations into metal. Firms as different in size as Honda and Laverda introduced full-sized motor-cycles with engines of such specific power as in early days had been associated only with the most rabid racing machinery, yet combined now with flexible quiet easy manners and even electric starters. Guzzi brought out a 700 cc tourer whose V-twin engine was transversely mounted and coupled to the rear wheel by shaft drive, an arrangement which must have inspired a good deal of interest in Munich; and then, in final confirmation of what was to come, two very different designs from BSA-Triumph and Honda made it clear that motor-cycling was back in a big way, and that in the upper strata of motor-cycling society a 750 cc engine would be the norm. Somebody called these newcomers *superbikes:* the name stuck, the idea took hold, and with a bit of help from a few proselytising journalists who were not content to preach only to the converted, motorcycle sales took off like a rocket.

Amidst all this, what were BMW doing? It did not look much, it did not look promising, indeed it looked little more than a pathetic attempt to gain sales (or gain time) by bowing to other people's standards and accepting other people's conventions. The R69S was modified for the American market, with a new gearbox and telescopic forks. There were at least some Englishmen who thought it merely unfortunate that this revised model should be known as the R69US . . .

If BMW wanted to stay alive they would have to look lively, or they would be trampled underfoot in the new rush; and liveliness was a deliberately cultivated characteristic of the new /5 series that was at last uncovered late in 1969. As much as possible and more than most, it was the /5 that was to be a motorcycle for gentlemen and without any doubt a motorcycle for the connoisseur. It was certainly not one that would satisfy the rider avid for ephemeral sensation, for it still felt like a luxury sporting tourer. It was still a quiet machine, very smooth, one that could be ridden hard and fast without attracting attention to itself—and therein lay much of its appeal, for it was essentially much more practical than some of its supposed rivals. An electric starter confirmed the practicality, though that infuriating ignition key plunger (almost the only item to survive from the old models) and a nearly invisible rev-counter conspired to deny it; but overall it remained what the BMW had long been thought—a machine to buy and keep for travelling long distances in decent comfort and at respectable speeds, rather than one to take out for the sheer fun of it. As a matter of course it was accepted that the essential BMW features should survive: the new engines were still transverse boxer twins, still with unit clutch and engine-speed input to the gearbox, still with shaft drive to the rear wheels. Otherwise everything was new, from the long-travel telescopic front forks to the upswept silencers; but paradoxically the novelties had the effect of making the newcomers look curiously old-fashioned. The short wheel-base, and the enclosure of all engine ancillaries in tall crankcase castings, combined to make the machine look high; a skinny front tyre on a big spidery front wheel, contrasting with a smaller rear wheel carrying a tyre that was less exiguous but could not yet be called wide, echoed the vaguely vintage air (with off-highway over-tones) that the Japanese were again making fashionable in the USA. With its engine tilted upwards to reduce drive-line angularity and increase cornering ground clearance, it looked like a self-castoring outboard with a broken back, or a rejected prop for an Easy Rider. As a glamorous motorcycle likely to appeal to currently (if inexplicably) fashionable American tastes, it carried a certain and rather commercial conviction; yet it somehow seemed less futuristic than the low, chunky, soft-mannered sobersides that it replaced.

Under the skin it was decidedly more up-to-date. The engine had been turned literally upside-down—and figuratively inside-out, for whereas the old one had been hefty outside and lightly built within, the new one with its light-alloy cylinder barrels and rugged crank-shaft was quite the opposite.

Lubrication was the nub of the matter. It was not just a matter of the camshaft being moved to the bottom of the engine beneath the crankshaft, with which it was linked by a spring-tensioned chain, though this inversion of former practice must have improved working conditions for the cams and tappets. Much more to the point was that instead of a flimsy flexible built-up crankshaft girt with rolling-element bearings, there was now a rigid one-piece affair, running in modern multilayer plain bearings and enjoying the luxury of an oil feed pumped at about 5.7 bars through a micromesh paper filter from an Eaton pump in the wet sump. It was almost an admission by the factory that the old 'bikes had given trouble.

The big ends in the old BMWs had been splash-lubricated with oil flung by centrifugal force from thrower plates, pressed steel saucers on the cheeks on the crankshaft webs. Rolling-element bearings do not need a lot of oil—indeed they are as likely to overheat by being supplied with too much as by being starved of it—so the oil pump could be a modest thing and the system pressure slight. It would have been all very well but for the development of sludge, which could fill the spinning saucers and divert the big-end's oil from its proper course. It did not always happen as a matter of course; but in some countries, depending on the climate and fuel and oil and usage, BMW owners had learned that big-end failure might occur at a mere forty or fifty thousand miles. Whether to strip the engine and clean it out at thirty-five thousand miles, or wait for the trouble that might never come, was always a difficult decision; and while there were riders generous with oil changes and throttle, knocking off equally generous mileages with no trouble at all, there were always enough disaffected sludgees to cast aspersions on the BMW reputation.

In any case, a roller bearing is quite the wrong kind for a big-end. The angular swing of the conrod makes the rollers accelerate and decelerate with every revolution, while their own inertia tries to constrain them to maintain a constant velocity, and the result is a perpetual skidding and scuffing that can be a distressingly brief prelude to a sudden and noisy failure. Much better to let little molecules of oil do the rolling, in well-fed hydrodynamic bearings—even if the things have to be split to be clamped around the journals on the one-piece crankshaft, introducing bolts to blinker the eyes of conrods that no longer looked uncommon.

The rods of the new /5 engines were common in ways that were significant. They were common to all the machines in the range, to the 500 cc R50/5, the 600 cc R60/5, and the 750 cc superbike that was numbered with equal inevitability. More to the point, the rods were common to the 2.8 litre six-cylinder engines of BMW's most potent current production car: they had the same bearings, enjoyed the same lubrication, and were less heavily loaded. They thus enjoyed ample reserves of strength and fatigue resistance, even in the 57SAE/50DIN horsepower R75/5, the power peak of which occurred at a surprisingly modest 6200 rpm. All three engines were virtually identical, the only differences being in bore and carburation and in minor variations in crankshaft balance controlled by small plates attached to the crank cheeks.

Perhaps the old-style crankshaft, with its roller bearings and built-up construction (which made up for its flimsiness with an inherent tendency to damp out torsional vibration) was adequate for its designed performance. The new forged crank and massive conrods were capable of handling far more than they were actually required to endure. What then had happened to the cost accounting procedures? Why this apparently lavish endowment? It could have been intended that these extra reserves of strength and stiffness would allow the development of more powerful engines in the future. More probably the costs had been very nicely calculated, and the conclusion reached that a single range of components that could remain unmodified for several years and serve the whole range, including any anticipated extensions of it, was worth the extra investment in crankshaft forging equipment, bearing in mind that the connecting rods were in production already for the cars.

This same long-sighted robustness was built into the whole of the transmission line, from the new diaphragm clutch to the final-drive bevel gear with built-in shock absorber. In particular the gearbox was a sturdy thing, with a new spring-loaded changing mechanism which had been introduced on the recent R69US. That transitional machine had, it will be recalled, been made to look more conventional and possibly more appealing by the adoption of telescopic front forks; and these figured large in the publicity for the new /5 series. The figures were 214 mm (nearly 8.5 in) of suspension travel from a fork weighing only 11.7 kg, compared with 14.5 kg for the Earles type. Given properly progressive spring rates there is no real need for

8 inches of fork plunge when riding upon ordinary roads, nor indeed much attraction in it when riding fast; but the Americans were demanding squashy suspension with which to ride off the highway, and since BMW had not broken themselves of the curious habit of subjecting their eminently unsuitable motorcycles to the indignities of roughriding competitions (indeed, the mighty Sebastian Nachtmann was very competitive on them), they were hardly in a position to argue. When it came to the test there was really no argument: with its trailing arm rear suspension increased in travel to 125 mm (from 105), and with weight-saving studied to such good purpose that the R75/5 was at least 10 kg lighter than the R69S despite the considerable strengthening of all major components, and despite even the addition of a hefty ½ horsepower electric starter, the new 'bikes would out-handle the old in virtually any circumstances.

As before, the frame was made up of a double loop with conical oval tubes, but it was now more compact, with a disturbingly light rear section merely bolted to the main frame. Elsewhere the joints were argon-welded, and very beautifully. This type of inert gas welding, sometimes called heliarc, needs special equipment and skills, but given them offers results far better than might be obtained by the techniques more familiar to motorcycle frame builders. More interesting than its strength, however, was the controlled stiffness of this frame: laterally it was fairly resistant to distortion, but longitudinally it was deliberately compliant, von der Marwitz believing then as now that too much stiffness is undesirable in a roadster frame, however appropriate it might be to a racer. In particular he was concerned about a shake originating as a lateral movement at the rear tyre and being transmitted through the frame to the steering head to emerge as a low-speed wobble: this had to be countered by strict tolerances in wheel construction and in lateral stiffness of the rear tyres. Responsibility for the latter was shared between Metzeler and Continental, the former achieving the desired results by the insertion of laminae of hard rubber in the tyre sidewalls, the latter achieving the same results by specialised carcass construction. There is evidence to suggest that selective testing of finished tyres was done, only the best being delivered to BMW for original equipment on their motorcycles; whether a rider might find replacement tyres as good when the time came to fit them was rather less certain than the probability that he would have steering troubles if he tried tyres of any other make or size.

He might equally run into trouble if he ignored the factory's advice and insisted on having high wide handlebars instead of the neat, narrow, and almost flat pattern supplied as a matter of course to European customers, a pattern which automatically imposed a slightly procumbent, beautifully balanced and fatigue-allaying riding position. Whether because of the greater moment of inertia created by the bigger handlebars, or because they imposed the kind of riding position which left the driver pulling on the bars instead of leaning on them, the result could be a high-speed steering shake of bone-melting severity. The steering damper was a necessary part of the specification.

Many owners rode happily and fairly quickly without ever noticing. The /5 series may not have been perfect, but they were a lot better than nearly all their rivals, and many owners were entranced by the agility of their handling, enhanced by the short wheelbase deliberately contrived to enliven steering response. It was a responsive and surprisingly sure-footed bicycle, and despite the big cylinders protruding from its flanks the R75 could be laid over further (and more quickly, since its weight was both less and lower) than any other 750 in showroom condition. It was quite an eye-opener, even if it was not yet up to the standard of the Manx Norton.

The Manx was of course a genuine racer, and the BMW was not as amenable to conversion to this rôle as some of its commercial rivals. When stripped and modified as far as racing regulations allowed (the extent depending on the country concerned), some of the rivals could be made much more raceworthy. Nevertheless the occasional really dashing rider, such as Germany's Helmut Dahne in Europe and expatriate Englishman Reg Pridmore in the USA, proved that it was possible to race very competitively on the /5 BMW.

Dahne is more surprising than his mount, an amateur who turns out only four times a year but is one of the finest and fastest production racers in Europe. Apart from a solitary outing in 1961 he started racing seriously in 1968, doing the national round of road-racing and hill-climbing on what was virtually a stripped R50 with a roller engine. Three years later came the R75/5 in production and Formula 750 guises; years later still, when he also had a very special 900 cc engine in his armoury, an open formula unit with titanium conrods, high-compression pistons, bigger valves, special camshaft, and close-ratio gears, he was still content to insert it in his old R75/5 frame, complete with its original roadster rear suspension and only slightly stiffened front forks.

The BMW ridden by Pridmore in American events was more extensively modified by Helmut Kern for its entrants Messrs. Butler and Smith, BMW distributors for the western States. Work started on a '71 model by fitting fancy tank and seat, a 19 inch rear rim, heavy-duty dampers and a sports camshaft. The wheel hubs were drilled and ventilated, and with the compression ratio slightly raised and the pedals moved aft, the 'bike was off to a good start. Much more followed in the course of securing fifteen wins and six second places out of twenty-three starts in two years, with never a failure to finish and never a place lower than third in what the Americans liked to think of as production racing. Like all good production racers, this BMW ended up a lot less standard than it looked, with a drilled flywheel, lightweight valvegear, and all manner of detailed refinements. The most interesting alteration was to increase cornering clearance by making the engine narrower from head to head: the secret was short connecting rods and special pistons that permitted the cylinder barrels themselves to be made shorter. With an extensively re-worked pair of front forks, featuring shorter travel and firmer damping, this BMW had an outstanding performance into and out of corners—and, like Dahne's machine, it was a bit short of brakes, for the standard drums were no bigger than those of the old R50. Unlike Dahne, however, Pridmore sometimes encountered that nasty wobble that was blamed on the short rear forks of the /5 series.

A longer wheelbase, mostly derived from longer rear forks, improved high-speed stability in the last of the /5 series, brought out early in 1973. Two of these late-model R75/5 BMWs were picked at random from the production line by the West German Motorcycling Federation, were run in under supervision, and then were shipped in sealed cases to the Isle of Man for an attempt sponsored by the British concessionaires to win the Maudes Trophy. This is awarded each year, if at all, for the best performance in a certified test carried out under ACU regulations and judging; and it is not given very often. The last occasion had been in 1963; now, fourteen riders were scheduled to keep these two machines running day and night around the open public roads constituting the TT circuit, for a week on end. When these roads are closed for racing they constitute a demanding circuit over which ten laps are considered a very long way indeed; when they are open to ordinary traffic and the motorcycles are not purposeful racers but ordinary production jobs, the demands are even more onerous. On this occasion, matters were made even worse by the fact that heavy rain fell for almost the whole week. To show how arduous it was, the riders were wearing out tyres in as little as a thousand miles, despite the wet roads; and at the end of seven days and nights, those two BMWs had completed 16,658 miles—and they won the Trophy.

Here was evidence that BMW reliability was at least as good as it had ever been. It was evidence too that standards were now gratifyingly high at the new Spandau factory, something that could not be said when the first /5 motorcycles came on the market. It had been earlier still, as early as 1966, that a start had been made on moving motor-cycle production to this factory near the Berlin Wall. With the car business booming, the company wanted all the factory space it could find around Munich, and more: they bought the Dingolfing premises of Glas, who had fallen on hard times despite producing some quite attractive coupés a couple of years earlier. The motorcycles, whether they were to be kept in production or phased out, had to be got out of the way, and Spandau looked like the place to do it. In the next five years 1½ million pounds were spent on tooling, and by 1971 everything except the crankshafts and gearboxes of the motorcycles was Berlin made. By the following year, those components too were produced at Spandau. There, an engine was completed every six minutes on a continually moving assembly line. Every finished engine was run for half an hour on the brake, with short bursts up to full throttle, with every two-hundredth engine being taken off the line and submitted to a more rigorous eight-hour test with long bouts of running wide open. Frame inspection was as rigorous, with a rejection rate occasionally reaching fourteen per cent and output nevertheless swelling all the time.

In the early 1970s BMW were not particularly happy about market trends. They could see that there was beginning to be a demand for something even bigger and more powerful, and that communicative engineer Dr Helmut Bönsch (now retired) declared that it would be a pity if the company had to defer to it.

Years later they are probably glad that they did. Late in 1973 came the /6 series, and with it the upward extension of the range that had so long been forecast. The little R50 had been dropped, and the top of the tree was now occupied by a brace of 900 cc BMWs, the R90/6 and the R90S.

The new range still all had the same stroke, the extra capacity being achieved by increasing bore diameter. The effect of this on volumetric efficiency was such that torque increased out of proportion to the increase in displacement, the two 900s differing but slightly: the S had a little more fierceness in its camshaft and rather unexpectedly wore Italian Dell'Orto carburettors, while the R90/6 kept the constant-vacuum Bing carburettors that had been standard on the R75/5. Most of the electrics had been uprated, including the alternator and battery, while the headlamp carried the H4 halogen bulb that had been such a success in the Maudes Trophy machines.

The new 'bikes had not merely been uprated, they had been extensively re-designed. One of the most important novelties was the much needed five-speed gearbox—not that the engines were in any way lacking in the spread of torque necessary to ensure adequate flexibility with the old four-speed box, but so as to improve the quality of the gearchange by increasing the number of steps with a view to making their increments smaller: the BMW gearchange had never been one of the easiest, and its difficulties were greatly abated by closer ratios. As it happened, many of these early five-speed boxes gave trouble, and some frantic comings and goings were necessary to ensure that all the rogues were identified, sent back to the factory, and corrected. When this had been done, the outcome was a box that could only justify serious criticism for the change from first to second gear, all the others being of perfectly acceptable quality with or without use of the clutch. In the case of the R90S, changing without the clutch was to be preferred: it was advisable to conserve the strength in one's fingers and forearm for the negotiation of town traffic or other circumstances where use of the particularly heavy clutch could not be avoided.

It was a little bit fierce, the S. It was high geared, high seated, a high-stepping thoroughbred with a touch of the mettlesome in its character. At high rpm the engine was as smooth as all the others; lower down, the big bangs in those high-compression cylinders could be felt; and not all of it was the detonation or pre-ignition that also affected the R60/6, a fault best corrected with electronic advance as with the Lucas Rita ignition apparatus. Pinking apart, the roughness of the S was not a vibration so much as a shake, a transverse pounding that made the surprisingly good low-speed pulling power of the engine a virtue that was more of academic interest than of practical utility.

Nor did the shakes end there. When the S was nudging the red sector of the dial with its rev-counter needle, at a true 128 mph after making corrections for centrifugal expansion of the tyres, the steering began that minatory weave, that nod which is as good as a wink to a blind man. The new frame had the same long wheelbase as the last of the /5 series, and its top tube had been stiffened, but still the steering damper was there to be used. In fact it was a new one, an improved version of the hydraulic damper first introduced in 1961 on the R69S. Something else was needed to cope with these high speeds too, and at long blessed last BMW had given us disc brakes. Only on the front wheels, mark you, and only as standard on the 750 and 900 models, though the disc was an option on the R60. The S carried twin discs on its front wheel, looking very handsome in stainless steel, with swing-out calipers behind the fork legs where they would interfere least with the steering and provide for easy wheel removal. It seemed a petty sort of economy that the R90/6, as substantial as the S and nearly as fast, should have only a single front disc; the availability of a twin as an option looked suspiciously like a palliative to whatever serves as a conscience in marketing men. In heavy rain, even the twin discs of the S were inadequate: in fact they were capable when soused of becoming completely impotent, and it was not until tangential drilling of the discs was introduced a couple of years later that this treachery was overcome.

Even more copious drilling of the brake discs fore *and aft* featured in the very special BMW that Butler & Smith were racing by this time in the USA, still with Reg Pridmore mastering it and Helmut Kern masterminding it. The 67 bhp of the production R90S paled by comparison with the 90 of this outrageously potent 750, more heavily modified than ever, but still based on standard BMW crankcase, cylinder, and head castings, and crankshaft forging. Least standard of all was the frame, a very stiff full-double-cradle affair of chromium molybdenum steel built by England's Rob North, the man who built similar and gloriously successful frames for the BSA and Triumph factory racers just a few years earlier. The wheelbase was a long 58 inches, nothing was supposed to flex, nothing was allowed to weigh more than it must, and when it was wearing the right tyres on its magnesium alloy wheels there were no complaints about its steering. This 310 lb paragon may still be the fastest pushrod-engined motorcycle in road racing.

If it is not, its rival must be the 1000 cc special developed from the R90S by Paul Blum for Hans Otto Butenuth, best known of all current BMW riders. This prodigious power unit is so lusty that full acceleration cannot be deployed in first or second gears because the torque strips the teeth off the pinions. In any case, Butenuth's real favourite is the dear old overhead-camshaft Rennsport engine, his pride and joy in racing since 1964 after an R51 had earned him his international licence a couple of years earlier. In 1971 he was the German champion, but his BMW then had a factory engine with centre bearing.

Such developments on the old overhead-cam engine were really kept up for the benefit of the sidecar racers, whose supremacy continued almost uninterrupted early in the 1970s. How much good it did the BMW reputation had long been debated, and in recent years it has been inevitable that most of the company's publicity-seeking is done in car racing: not more than three per cent of the BMW racing budget is spent on motorcycles, and not much of that now goes into the Rennsport engines. Nevertheless BMW think that it would be a shame to disappear from this scene that has for so long been so peculiarly their own: after a whole generation relying on the old grand prix engines, with only spares being manufactured since, they have allowed development technician Rudolph Helser to evolve a new engine with three main bearings and with four valves in each cylinder head. It is by no means as powerful as the most rabid of the current racing two-strokes, but at least it is as powerful when hot as when cool, which is more than can be said for them.

It is all slightly irrelevant, for it has been a long time since BMW motorcycles were built to accept sidecars. Their frames are far too weak around the rear fork anchorage—possibly too weak for solo machines, let alone for combinations. Nevertheless, the chassis of the /6 series did enjoy some improvement late in 1975, the most notable modification being a stiffening of the front forks; but changes in the engine and gearbox were more numerous, including stronger crankcases, more rigid camshaft mounting, more substantial cylinder barrels, and a stronger gearbox. The whole range has profited from these modifications, and are now to be seen as very well behaved bicycles indeed, though with its extra power and more violent reactions the S can still show the cloven hoof.

As far as the world at large is concerned, including all but a tiny minority of riders who push the 'bike to its limits, the R90S showed the flag for BMW. Its idiosyncratic appearance confirms this intention: this was the first BMW to enjoy the attentions of a stylist, when a new position was created in the motorcycle division for that kind of industrial designer and a newcomer called Hans Muth was brought in from Ford to fill it. His was the little fairing, the luxurious seat, the instrumentation (complete with a fine clock, the first on a production motorcycle since the long-lamented Ariel Leader); and his was the very fancy air-brushed paint scheme that made every individual S a different, hand-finished, *unique* motorcycle. For Muth it was a tentative start; what he did next was carried out with far more conviction, was literally and figuratively of much greater moment.

	R50/5	R60/5	R75/5
ENGINE Type Number	246	246	246
Cylinders, bore, stroke mm	2x67x70.6	2x73.5x70.6	2x82x70.6
Displacement cm^3	498	599	745
Compression ratio :1	8.6	9.2	9
Valve location	oh	oh	oh
Camshaft(s)	1	1	1
Carburettor(s)	2 Bing 26mm	2 Bing 26mm	2 Bing 32mm CD
Power PS max	32	40	50
at rev/min	6400	6400	6200
Corresponding bmep kg/cm^2	9.16	9.52	9.88
Oil capacity, litres	2	2	2
TRANSMISSION Type Number	246	246	246
Gear ratios :1 i	2.60	2.60	2.60
top gear ii	1.72	1.72	1.72
iii	1.25	1.25	1.25
iv	1	1	1
Final drive ratio :1	3.56	3.36	2.91
CHASSIS Type Number	246	246	246
Frame	tubular cradle with bolted-on rear sub-frame		
Front forks	telescopic	telescopic	telescopic
springing	internal helical	internal helical	internal helical
damping	hydraulic, double-acting	hydraulic, double-acting	hydraulic, double-acting
Rear forks	trailing fork	trailing fork	trailing fork
springing	helical, adjustable multi-rate		
damping	hydraulic	hydraulic	hydraulic
Front brake type	drum 2LS	drum 2LS	drum 2LS
diameter mm	200	200	200
Rear brake type	drum 1LS	drum 1LS	drum 1LS
Tyres	3.25S19F/4.00S18R		
Fuel tank, litres	22	22	22
Weight, kg	185	190	190
Maximum speed km/h	157	167	175
Frame numbers	2900001-2903623	2930001-2938704	2970001-2982737
Engine numbers	2900001-2903623	2930001-2938704	2970001-2982737
Quantity built	7865	22721	38370
Years of Production	1969—73	1969—73	1969—73

	R60/6	R75/6	R90/6
ENGINE Type Number	247	247	247
Cylinders, bore, stroke mm	2x73.5x70.6	2x82x70.6	2x90x70.6
Displacement, cm^3	599	745	898
Compression ratio :1	9.2	9	9
Valve location	oh	oh	oh
Camshaft(s)	1	1	1
Carburettor(s)	2 Bing 26mm	2 Bing 32mm CD	2 Bing 32mm CD
Power PS max	40	50	60
at rev/min	6400	6200	6500
Corresponding bmep kg/cm^2	9.52	9.88	9.38
Oil capacity, litres	2	2	2
TRANSMISSION Type Number	247	247	247
Gear ratios :1 i	2.93	2.93	2.93
ii	1.91	1.91	1.91
iii	1.38	1.38	1.38
iv	1.11	1.11	1.11
Final drive ratio :1	3.36	3.2	3.09
CHASSIS Type Number	247	247	247
Frame	tubular cradle with bolted-on rear sub-frame		
Front forks	telescopic	telescopic	telescopic
springing	internal helical	internal helical	internal helical
damping	hydraulic, double-acting	hydraulic, double-acting	hydraulic, double-acting
Rear forks	trailing fork	trailing fork	trailing fork
springing	helical, adjustable multi-rate		
damping	hydraulic	hydraulic	hydraulic
Front brake type	drum 2LS	disc	disc
diameter mm	200	260	260
Rear brake type	drum 1LS	drum 1LS	drum 1LS
Tyres	3.25S19F/4.00S182		3.25H19F/4.00H18
Fuel tank, litres	18	18	18
Weight, kt	200	200	200
Maximum speed km/h	167	177	188
Frame numbers	2910001—	4010001—	4040001—
Engine numbers	2910001—	4010001—	4040001—
Quantity built	13511	17587	21097
Years of Production	1973—6	1973—6	1973—6

R90S

ENGINE	Type Number	247
Cylinders, bore, stroke mm		2x90x70.6
Displacement cm^3		898
Compression ratio :1		9.5
Valve location		oh
Camshaft(s)		1
Carburettor(s)		2 Dell'Orto 38mm
Power PS max		67
at rev/min		7000
Corresponding bmep kg/cm^2		9.73
Oil capacity, litres		2

TRANSMISSION	Type Number	247
Gear ratios :1	i	2.93
	ii	1.91
	iii	1.38
	iv	1.11
Final drive ratio :1		3

CHASSIS	Type Number	247
Frame		tubular cradle with bolted-on rear subframe
Front forks		telescopic
springing		internal helical
damping		hydraulic, double-acting
Rear forks		trailing fork
springing		helical, adjustable multi-rate
damping		hydraulic
Front brake type		2 disc
diameter mm		260
Rear brake type		drum 1LS
Tyres		3.25H19F/4.00H18R
Fuel tank, litres		24
Weight, kg		205
Maximum speed km/h		200+
Frame numbers		4070001-
Engine numbers		4070001-
Quantity built		17455
Years of Production		1973—6

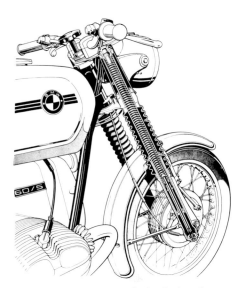

Long-stroke telescopic forks declared more explicitly than any other feature the return to orthodoxy that governed the design of the /5 series.

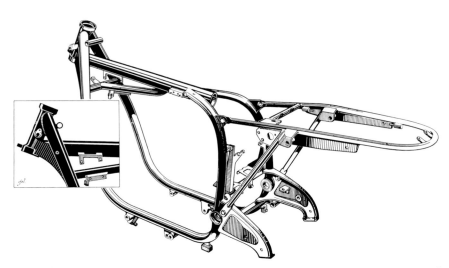

The /5 frame was fashion-conscious, but the steering head was better braced than fashion required.

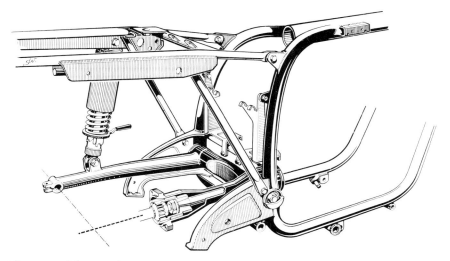

The rear subframe of the /5 was merely a bolt-on sub-assembly.

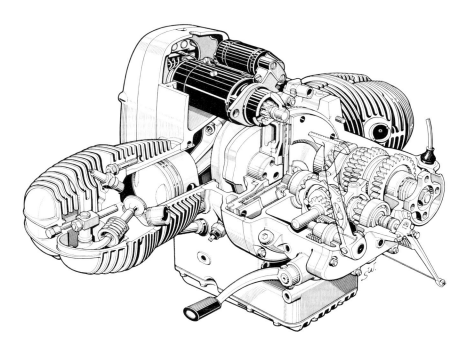

Plain bearings and fancy liners were two features of the /5 engines.

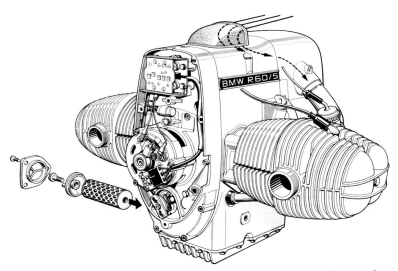

The front chest of the 1971 series /5 engines housed diode rectifier, condensor, 12V/180W alternator, and contact-breaker. Also indicated are the intake air flow and the oil filter.

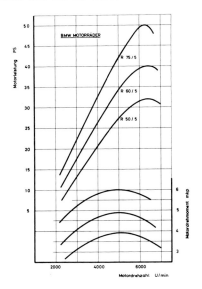

Power (Leistung, in metric horsepower or PS) and torque (Drehmoment, in metre kiloponds) curves for the /5 engines.

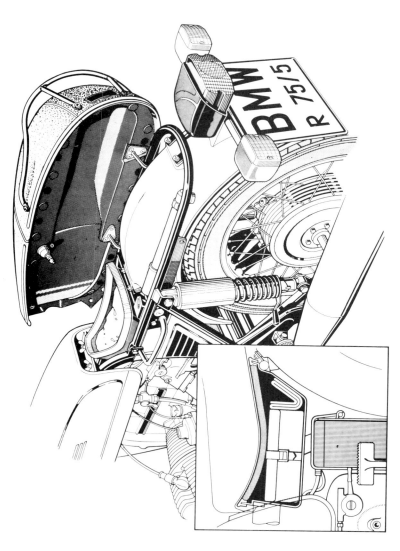

Amidst all the flash and glitter of the 1971 /5 BMWs was some good detail, including the saddle-sealed toolchest, the push-on pump, and easily-cleaned lamps.

Much more purposeful was this cross-country prototype version of the R75/5: built in 1970, it very nearly went into production.

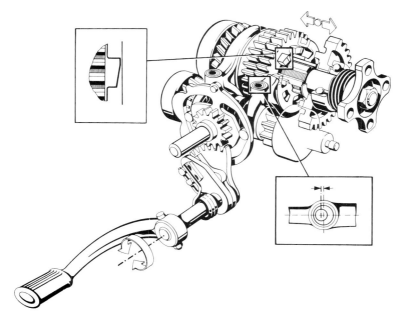

Four-speed gearbox of the /5 series.

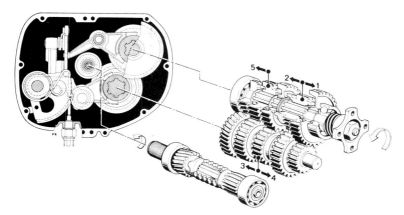

One of the greatest improvements in the /6 was the five-speed gearbox, its three-shaft layout better elaborated here than in earlier drawings.

The other great boon of the /6 was the disc front brake, prominent on this R75 being assayed by the author shortly before its public debut.

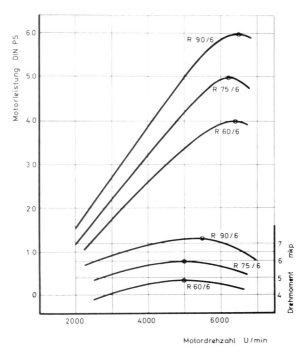

Power and torque curves for the /6 series tourers.

Three-position hydraulic damper (off/soft/hard) on the /6.

R90/6

R90S, the sportster with screen, fairing and double discs as standard.

In the lee of the R90S screen lay voltmeter, clock (hurrah!), speedometer and rev-counter, along with assorted admonitions and warning lights.

Two 260mm discs and swing-out calipers on the R90S. Perforations came later and were necessary in wet weather.

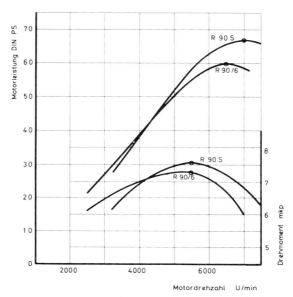

R90S sportster and R90/6 tourer reveal their characters in their curves.

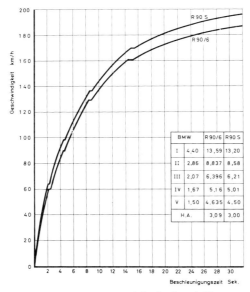

BMW	R90/6	R90 S
I	4,40	13,59	13,20
II	2,86	8,837	8,58
III	2,07	6,396	6,21
IV	1,67	5,16	5,01
V	1,50	4,635	4,50
H.A.		3,09	3,00

Different gearing amplified the differences in performance.

Without looking very non-standard, the R90S could be quite effective as a production racer.

CHAPTER 7

A SENSE OF PERMANENCE

It is generally supposed to take three generations to make a gentleman. How a generation is measured in the life of a motorcycle you may decide for yourself; but BMW have been evolving their own pure-bred line for long enough now, and there can be no doubt that the latest series display the most impeccable manners. Here at last in the /7 series is a BMW that does not need and does not have (except apparently for cosmetic purposes on the RS model) a steering damper, a BMW that was pronounced by that prince of racers, Phil Read, to be completely stable right up to the onset of wheelspin at 190 km/h in pouring rain when he was first to try the R100RS at a journalists' pre-release test day, before the new range of machines was proclaimed to an expectant public in September 1976. It was not just the new bracing around the steering head that was responsible for this new access of high-speed dirigibility, which in better circumstances extends right through to the 200 km/h (124 mph) or more that the RS can reach. A good deal of aerodynamic subtlety, peculiar to the new fairing that is the unique proposition of the RS, has a lot more to do with it. Nor is it necessarily the dimensional uniformity and lateral stiffness of the cast aluminium-alloy wheels: despite their attractions they are optional equipment, and the RS behaves well enough without them. Rather it is the product of many pieces of detail development, such as the reinforcement of the rear forks to provide greater strength and torsional stiffness.

Nor indeed are these boons only to be enjoyed at high speeds and on motorway straights, for at the other extreme the modern BMW is even more praiseworthy. The rate at which these cobby twins can be cranked from a hairpin *this* way to a hairpin *that* way is a revelation, after some of the blundering Behemoths offered by other manufacturers who would like to think themselves rivals, but have not enough generations behind them to make them even contemporaries.

More astonishing still is the modern BMW's disregard for bumps. It is not merely a rider's desire to cosset his posterior that makes this important: it matters when a patch of road that looks to be full of puddles turns out on arrival at 80 mph to be full of potholes, when all one can do is rise in the stirrups, keep the throttles open and await safe deliverance at the other end. It matters on those Alpine passes where one has the choice of taking a proper line through a tight corner and risking being thrown off into the valley below by the terribly uneven surface near the edge of the road, just where one wants to clip it; or taking a different line in the middle of the road where the going is smoother, but one which gives less margin for error if it turns wet in the shade or if something comes the other way . . . in which case it may still be the valley in the end. Here one may safely choose the bumpy way, and with the BMW heeled right over it might not be surprising were it to shake its head instead of simply going, as it does, where it is steered. It matters in dense urban traffic, where it is not always possible to choose a line uncorrupted by manhole covers, raised white lines, and the depredations of the Gas Board's ditch-diggers, where to be thrown off course may mean being thrown off entirely.

Such virtues are rare, particularly among the few big bangers that can rival the performance of these modern BMWs. Can one put a price on these virtues? Can one say that good finish is worth so much, perfectly spaced gear ratios a bit more, shaft drive another couple of hundred and a tenner extra for the clock? One cannot. I refuse to be drawn into any argument about whether the R100RS in particular or any modern BMW in general is worth its very high price. All that can be said is that it is probably the best production motorcycle in the world, and if that is the price of it then either you can afford it or you cannot. What I think more interesting is to consider whether it is yet as good as it could be, as good as a BMW should be after 54 years practice.

The answer must be negative. All motorcycles are still old-fashioned, and so is the BMW. It still scores over all the others by offering the best modern details (brakes, electrics and the like) and yet keeping such good old-fashioned virtues as quality, moderate weight, low centre of gravity, good finish and easy handling. Nevertheless I am convinced that BMW could make a much more modern and much cleverer machine if they wanted to.

It seems that they do not. In front of them all the time is the BMW image, a purely notional and therefore unbreakable ikon which determines how a BMW motorcycle must look, how it may sound, what it should feel like and even approximately how much it should cost. It must be recognisably a BMW, and that means shaft drive, a transverse flat-twin engine, a soft well-damped ride, a looped tubular frame, and all those other truths that the Bavarian constitution holds self-evident.

There is—always accepting the premises of a traditional design rather than some farfetched stressed-skin link-steered aerodyne, which some day I should like to see and which some day Dr Dietrich Reister (head of motorcycle development, and currently planning for production in the 1980s) may produce—a good deal of sense in this BMW recipe. Shaft drive, for example, ought no longer to be exceptional. One look at the absurdity of the enormous and exposed chain links on the latest big Kawasaki or Laverda ought to suffice to convert anyone; but there is a further point, for the forces that have to be countered in the design of a shaft-drive rear fork are so much more complex than those involved in a chain drive that the job simply has to be done properly. In other words I would trust almost anybody's shaft-drive rear end not to distort, but I would trust nobody's chain-driven end.

Shaft drive is mechanically wasteful if the engine's crankshaft be not longitudinal, for every extra right angle means a couple of per cent of torque down the drain. For years people objected to longitudinal crankshafts, saying that their torque reaction interfered with a 'bike's handling. The R90S could respond with the occasional nudge to a ferocious snap change-up while accelerating hard and banked well over, and any of them might go a little agley if one were to miss a gear in mid-corner: the fact is that torque reactions are going to affect the machine somehow, whichever way the engine be placed in the frame, but only the most sudden variations of great amplitude matter in the slightest, and such variations can be just as destabilising through pitch change in a motorcycle with a transverse crankshaft.

There is also the gyroscopic effect of the flywheel to be considered: again it is going to affect the 'bike somehow, whatever the plane of the flywheel—but again it is only rapid changes that matter. In fact gyroscopic precession of the flywheel is more likely to disturb the heading of a motorcycle with its crankshaft athwartships when the rider banks it quickly over, a situation in which the BMW layout remains immune from interference.

It does not necessarily follow that an opposed twin is the only suitable engine for the job. Ask any Porsche owner: the perfect balance of the flat twin can be extended to four or more cylinders, at the same time reducing the overall width of the engine. Herr von der Marwitz knows this as well as anybody, having come from work on Porsche engines; but he disapproves of the idea strongly, on the grounds that proper reliable cooling of the rear cylinders of a flat four would demand liquid cooling, and that that kind of sophistication is foreign to the proper spirit of a motorcycle.

The fact remains that those two big cylinders do stick out rather a long way, and it is possible to ground them when riding energetically, though only three or four times have I been brave enough to achieve those marks of distinction on the rocker boxes. Moreover, if the cylinders are more prominent than the rider's feet, they are adding to frontal area unnecessarily, not to mention increasing the polar moment of inertia in the banking plane.

While on the question of frontal area, an examination of the unparalleled range of BMW fairings is desirable. It is axiomatic that a square foot of frontal area is worth acres of aerodynamics, but it is no less valid an argument that a good fairing is worth a suit of clothes and a hot bath. BMW claim to be the only motorcycle manufacturer in the world to offer a complete range of fairings for all purposes, but only with the arrival of the R100RS does the range begin to look persuasive. Hitherto it consisted of three: the light touring windshield, fit only for light touring; the full fairing favoured by police forces and kindred authorities all over the world, a noisy and clumsy piece of claptrap that suffers from vortex shedding on alternate flanks at high speeds, producing a disconcerting wobble; and the ultra-light miniature fairing that set new fashions when it was integrated with the instruments and appurtenances around the handlebars of the R90S. What do we make of·that one?

There is no questioning the advantages of having something behind which to relax at high speeds, instead of working the neck muscles into a passable imitation of *rigor mortis*. But the screen of the 90S was only about 5 inches high, and did very little to take the brunt of a 120 mph headwind. Why was it made so small, unless for the improper reason that a large one would be murderous if attached to the forks and turning with them? A fairing should not be attached to the forks and turned with them, though it must be accepted that a little flyscreen is better than nothing, and one with a clock in it is better still. There remains a need for a full fairing integrated with the frame, shaped so as fully to protect the rider, so as to minimise drag by whatever compromises produce the lowest CdA—the product of drag coefficient multiplied by frontal area—and at the same time it should be so shaped as to induce no destabilising aerodynamic forces.

It is this last requirement which has hitherto been conspicuously ignored. All motorcycles are prey to a nose-up pitch increasing with speed, because the centre of anterior wind pressure is higher than the centre of gyration in the pitching plane. Most fairings, far from developing a negative lift or positive down-thrust to alleviate this tendency, aggravate it instead, so that as a high-performance motorcycle goes faster and faster, its front comes up higher and higher until the front suspension is at full droop, the steering rake and trail are travesties of their designed figures, the front tyre is barely touching the road and is unable to contribute much to good order and navigational discipline, and it only needs a little extra acceleration to lift the front of the 'bike completely clear of the ground. Is it any wonder that, with steering geometry and tyre response thus betrayed, so many motorcycles become incorrigible rogues at high speeds?

It only needs a little imagination, a little engineering ability, and perhaps a flow-visualisation test or two, to produce a fairing that induces an aerodynamic down-force that increases with speed to balance this natural nose-lifting tendency, so that the load borne by the front tyre (and the pitch attitude of the motorcycle as a whole) remain constant over the whole speed range. Muth and von der Marwitz did better than that: they hired the Pininfarina wind tunnel, the finest available to automotive engineers in Europe, at £2,600 a day, and did the job thoroughly. The fairing of the R100RS is a piece of very careful work: the integrated spoiler, the inclined head-lamp cover lying flush with the streamlining so as to avoid sharp edges that might interfere with the designed airflow, the flush turn-indicator lamps, the carefully ducted cooling for the engine, combined with the mirrors and the thorough hand protection to improve stability at high speeds and riding comfort at all speeds. The need to ensure the best possible vision in the worst imaginable circumstances dictated that the rider's eyes should look over the top of the steeply sloping polycarbonate windscreen, but the airflow over it at speed is such as to carry raindrops and other airborne flotsam up and over his helmet, rather than flinging it in his face. What did we say in Chapter 1? *Shed no tears for Johnny head-in-air* . . .

The man with his feet on the ground wants quantification of results. Muth and von der Marwitz both told me that the fairing succeeded in neatly nullifying lift to maintain a virtually constant load on the front wheel at all speeds, but publicity material issued by BMW when the new models were announced declared a reduction in front wheel lift of 17.4%. This is an extraordinarily precise figure, surely more precise than the margins of experimental error and verification; but whoever is right, the RS fairing is still a great advance over any other—especially taking further into account the claimed reduction in drag of 5.4% and in the yawing moment in side winds by no less than 60%. All this from a finely finished structure weighing only 9.5 kg (20.9 lb) cannot fail to be a bargain.

The advantages conferred by this stability are more numerous than the obvious ones. The BMW may be an aristocrat of motor-cycles, but now that it no longer goes around with its nose in the air its suspension can be given much better poise. The rule-of-thumb mechanics who play with extravagantly long spring travel may safely and even profitably be ignored: the proper way to ensure optimum ride comfort and handling, to allow the wheels to respond to the slightest rugosity of road surface yet deal firmly with the most vicious of humps and hollows, is to provide fully progressive springing. BMW have not gone that far yet, but the rear springing of the /7 series is an approximation to progressive rate in being dual-rate, pursuing a practice established in the days of the R69. Over the first two thirds of total travel (that is, 90 mm or 3.5 inches) the combined rate of the two rear springs is 16 kg/cm (89.4 lb/in) and this rises to 45 kg/cm (251.5 lb/in) in the last third of the movement towards full bump position. The three-position adjustment available is much as before— indeed the /7 series BMWs are paradoxical in appearing in some respects new but not different, in others different but not new. This state of affairs usually suggests the activity of stylists, and it is not hard to see supporting evidence in the new machines, notably in the novel polygonal rocker boxes. In many cases it is a matter of industrial design rather than artistic fancy, however: the finning of the cylinder barrels, for example, is thicker and shallower, improving the temperature gradients and therefore the heat dissipation and at the same time quietening fin vibration. Likewise the more massive proportions of the silicon-aluminium crankcase reinforce it to with-stand higher combustion and inertia forces—and the latter in particular must be expected, now that cylinder displacement in the biggest BMWs has risen to a full litre.

Basically the /7 series comes in three engine sizes, the R60/7, the R75/7, and the R100/7 which replaces the erstwhile R90/6. Elaborations of the biggest are the R100S, which bears an inflated correspondence to the former R90S, and the R100RS which is, we have seen, a new extension of the concept of a luxury high-performance motorcycle. The hyperventilation of the old 900 cc engine has been achieved as intended without altering the piston stroke, only the bore dimension being amplified to 94 mm; and with no other change it was to be expected that power need not be greater, though torque would undoubtedly be more grandiloquent. Thus it proves, for the R100S is actually 2 bhp down on the R90S, but both it and the particularly flexible R100/7 develop massive torque over a remarkably wide engine speed range, the softer-tuned of the two realising its maximum bmep at only 4000 rpm, and little less between 3500 and 5500. Larger-diameter intake and exhaust tracts enable the engine of the R100RS to sing up to 7250 rpm to develop its maximum of 70 bhp; and its song has a higher *tessitura*, with maximum bmep and torque on a plateau between 5300 and 6300 rpm. Interestingly, the higher revving of the RS has prompted the choice of a lower final-drive ratio than on the S.

To reach the maximum speed of this fastest of the new series, the rider of the RS will need to get down to it a little and tuck his head behind the screen. The seat is beautifully adapted to the appropriate posture, having a humped back that primarily serves as an aerodynamic complement to the fairing, a wake-filling extension of the rider's posterior. It is cushioned over a greater length than a solo racing-style seat, but it is hardly long enough to seat two. BMW are content with this, calling it a one-plus-half, and leaving it to local licensing authorities to decide whether it would be legal for the carriage of a pillion passenger. People in West Germany like to be disciplined and the authorities are only too happy to oblige, and their bureaucrats have determined that there is only room for one German: the pillion footrests are accordingly removed for that market. Doubtless the French will continue to pursue their policy of *laisser faire,* and the English as usual will let things slide—a rather unfortunate expression in this context. It does however prompt recollection of the slippery seats on the /5 and /6 series (other than the R90S) which were grippy enough if the rider were dressed in leather, but threatened to leave him behind if he gunned the engine while wearing nylon trousers.

In any case, the BMW in its more recent forms has always looked much more convincing as a bicycle built for one. It is not only the extravagant racers of Butenuth, Dahne and Pridmore that deserve to be noted, but also the multitude of production and endurance racers that have been seen on circuits far and wide. A few minor modifications, some clip-on handlebars, rear-set pedals, and a racing hump-backed seat, transform the normally placid looks of these urbane tourers, which in more ferocious guise have often performed well enough to surprise racier-looking opposition, while making a lot less noise about it. In the process they are often run to far higher crankshaft rates than the makers would recommend their ordinary customers to indulge—and some lessons must have been learned in the process, for the valvegear has been substantially improved in the /7 series, the pushrods now being made of aluminium alloy tube, while modifications to the rocker arms and tightening of valve-spring tolerances have helped to increase the engine's capacity for revolution, and at the same time contrive to ensure that as in the most civilised of societies, each revolution should be a quiet one.

However fast and fashion-conscious, the new BMWs are beyond question the most civilised yet, from Spandau or Munich or indeed anywhere else. Detail finish, overall balance, the feel of controls, the positive ease of the transmission, and not least the fact that the RS in particular can be ridden fast without much muscular exertion, without mechanical respite, and without having to be refuelled every 50 minutes—all the little things and the big ones combine to make these absolutely top-class motorcycles, pointers to a dicyclic civilisation to which we may still aspire. The little things are the things that change from year to year, from series to series; the big things as often as not are the things that are implicit in the idea of a BMW motorcycle.

At the beginning of this book we left Sir Kenneth Clark in the middle of a valiant attempt to define the quality of civilisation. *Civilisation means something more than energy and will and creative power . . . How can I define it? Well, very shortly a sense of permanence.* It is even so with the BMW motorcycle, something that has come through at least three generations and is now fit to be taken anywhere. Its upbringing has been accompanied by a flair for self-criticism, a sense of responsibility that may have extended the development time of some models considerably and some models too much, so that on occasions a finally matured design came too late to market. The BMW scooter was one of these, technically streets ahead of the happy-go-lucky machines which caused so much hilarious social upheaval in the late 1950s, but temporally miles behind in its commercial career. Back in 1934 there was another which was well ahead of its time, but nevertheless failed to arrive, the R7 with its elegantly engineered bridge frame onto which the engine was flanged from below. Perhaps it does not matter now: in a world of automotive ephemera, BMW have acquired their mastery of motorcycle building by steadily applying basic principles to a set of equally fundamental problems, neither of which has ever really changed since they began building in 1920. Ever since founder Friz produced what we could still call the modern BMW as a complete *Gestalt*, with its transverse boxer twin engine and shaft drive setting the pattern for the next 53 years or more, there have been changes. See for example how telescopic forks came and went only to return again, how long-range tanks have gone in and out of fashion, how the trimmings and trappings of the /5 and /6 series altered from year to year. In each case, after the first novelty had worn off, one hardly noticed the difference. Permanence is the thing.

	R60/7	R75/7	R100/7
ENGINE Type Number			
Cylinders, bore, stroke mm	2x73.5x70.6	2x82x70.6	2x94x70.6
Displacement cm^3	599	745	980
Compression ratio :1	9.2	9	9
Valve location	oh	oh	oh
Camshaft(s)	1	1	1
Carburettor(s)	2 Bing 26mm	2 Bing 32 mm CD	2 Bing 32 mm CD
Power PS max	40	50	60
at rev/min	6400	6200	6500
Corresponding bmep kg/cm^2	9.52	9.88	8.60
Oil capacity, litres	2	2	2
TRANSMISSION Type Number			
Gear ratios :1 i	2.93	2.93	2.93
top gear ii	1.91	1.91	1.91
iii	1.39	1.39	1.39
iv	1.11	1.11	1.11
v	1	1	1
Final drive ratio :1	3.36 or 3.56	3.20 or 3.36	3.09 or 3.20
CHASSIS Type Number			
Frame	tubular cradle with bolted-on rear subframe		
Front forks	telescopic	telescopic	telescopic
springing	internal helical	internal helical	internal helical
damping	hydraulic, double-acting	hydraulic, double-acting	hydraulic, double-acting
Rear forks	trailing fork	trailing fork	trailing fork
springing	helical, adjustable multi-rate		
damping	hydraulic	hydraulic	hydraulic
Front brake type	perforated disc	perforated disc	perforated disc
diameter mm	260	260	260
Rear brake type	drum 1LS	drum 1LS	drum 1LS
Tyres	3.25B19 f; 4.00B 18 r		
Fuel tank, litres	24 (3 reserve)	24 (3 reserve)	24 (3 reserve)
Weight, kg	195	195	195
Maximum speed km/h	164	176	185
Years of Production	1976–	1976–	1976–

			R100S	R100RS
ENGINE Type Number				
Cylinders, bore, stroke mm			2x94x70.6	2x94x70.6
Displacement cm^3			980	980
Compression ratio :1			9.5	9.5
Valve location			oh	oh
Camshaft(s)			1	1
Carburettor(s)			2 Bing 40mm CD	2 Bing 40mm CD
Power PS max			65	70
at rev/min			6600	7250
Corresponding bmep kg/cm^2			9.17	8.99
Oil capacity, litres			2	2
TRANSMISSION Type Number				
Gear ratios :1		i	2.93	2.93
top gear		ii	1.91	1.91
		iii	1.39	1.39
		iv	1.11	1.11
		v	1	1
Final drive ratio :1			2.91 or 3.00	3.00 or 2.91
CHASSIS Type Number				
Frame			tubular cradle with bolted-on rear subframe	
Front forks			telescopic	telescopic
springing			internal helical	internal helical
damping			hydraulic, double-acting	hydraulic, double-acting
Rear forks			trailing fork	trailing fork
springing			helical, adjustable multi-rate	
damping			hydraulic	hydraulic
Front brake type			2 perforated disc	2 perforated disc
diameter mm			260	260
Rear brake type			drum 1LS	drum 1LS
Tyres			3.25B19 f; 4.00B18 r	
Fuel tank, litres			24 (3 reserve)	24 (3 reserve)
Weight, kg			200	210
Maximum speed km/h			200	200
Years of Production			1976—	1976—

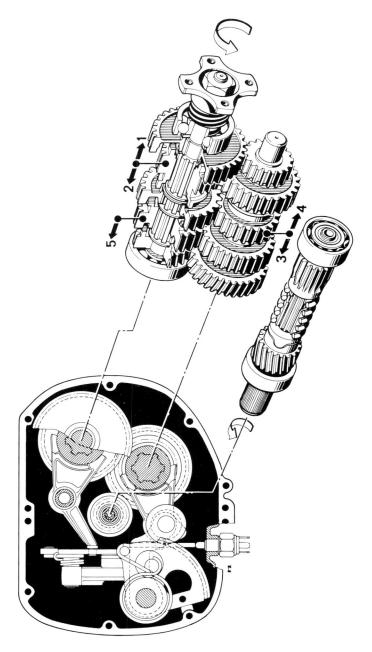

Best change yet: the 5-speed 3-shaft /7 gearbox.

Details on the /7 BMWs: distant early warning (by Fiamm), a flush screw-in collision-proof fuel tank bung (by order?).

The blackleg.

Wings make the switches easy to thumb.

The light-alloy wheels of the R100RS are an optional extra; everything else in these views is standard.

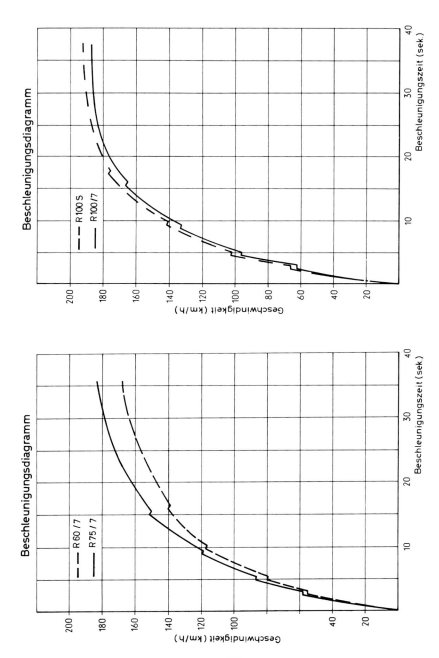

Acceleration curves for the four ordinary /7 models . . .

188

Beschleunigungsdiagramm

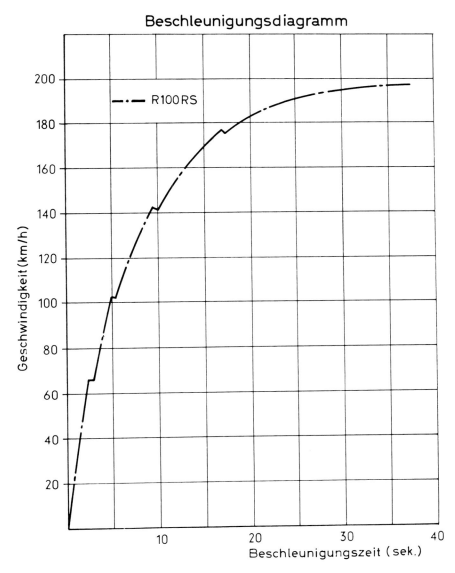

. . should be compared with that for the extraordinary R100RS, which begins
to outperform the R100S beyond 170 km/h.

And now go back and look again at the R32; or would you rather look forward?